ROBERT
THE
DOLL

COPYRIGHT NOTICE

WARNING

Robert is an antique doll on display at the Fort East Martello Museum in Key West, Florida. Many people believe that he is haunted. Reports of hauntings are certainly subjective, but accidents, mishaps, bad luck, misfortune, physical injury, and even deaths have been attributed to Robert the Doll.

This book is designed to provide information and entertainment to the reader. If you are sensitive to subjects of a paranormal nature, suffer from pediophobia (the fear of dolls) or night terrors, or are prone to delusional behavior, continue at your own risk.

Phantom Press, David L. Sloan, and The Key West Art & Historical Society shall not be liable for any physical, psychological, emotional, financial or commercial damages to readers, including, but not limited to, special, incidental, consequential, or other damages.

Enjoy.

March 31, 2010

Dear Robert:

I am very sorry for not asking your permission to take your picture while visiting the museum last week. Since I have taken your picture without permission, many strange things have happened to me.

While driving back from the Keys, a deer ran out in front of our car. We had to swerve to avoid hitting it, and ran off the road. We almost hit a tree.

Two days later, we had a small kitchen fire. Also, we have been hearing childlike giggles coming from our basement.

Last night, I was home all alone. I heard a voice coming from the basement. When I went to investigate, I tripped and fell down the bottom three stairs. I got up to run out, but the door was locked. My husband said that I probably turned the lock myself without even thinking about it and locked myself in the basement, but honestly, Robert, we both know the truth.

Please accept my deepest apology for taking your picture without asking. Also, please accept my daughter's apology for sticking out her tongue at you and making fun of you.

Sincerely,

4

"Be careful of the objects you possess,
or one day they may end up possessing you."
~ David Sloan

CHAPTERS

FEATURES

Dear Robert...
Letters to a haunted doll

Tales From The Turret
Artist House hauntings

Robert Did It!
Firsthand accounts

PREFACE

I didn't do it. Robert did it!

Hundreds of people gather each night for ghost tours to hear tales of Robert the Doll. He is regularly featured on television and is the star of hundreds of web sites. Robert is frequently sought out by psychics and paranormal investigators, receives more letters in a month than most of us receive in a year, and understandably tops lists of the most haunted dolls in the world. But what is it about this doll that sets him apart from the others? What makes Robert tick?

There are as many stories about Robert as there are letters in his mailroom at the Fort East Martello Museum. The stories range from terrifying to ridiculous, with varying degrees of believability. Most stories agree that Robert was created around the turn of the century and given as a gift to a young boy in Key West, but from this point the stories go in many directions. One commonality exists in every version of the tale: Robert has abilities not normally associated with inanimate objects.

When I first met Robert, he was not a star. It was 1996: only a handful of ghost tours existed in the United States, people still used film in their cameras, and *Newsweek* had recently published an article called "Why The Internet Will Fail."

I saw a ghost tour in Scotland and decided to start one of my own in Key West, but the venture got off to a slow start. Ask a local today where the haunted houses in Key West are located, and they are likely rattle off half a dozen locations less than a few blocks away. In 1996, ghosts were off the radar. No one talked about them much, no one wrote books about them, and few knew about them, apart from those who lived in the haunted homes. I only discovered Key West's ghost files in the library archives after several weeks of digging, when I was close to giving up.

I first heard Robert's name during a visit to the Key West guest house called the Artist House. I was hoping to confirm stories of Anne Otto's ghost (Anne Otto was the former owner of the house) and so I met with Darryl Meyer, who owned the guest house at the time.

"I'm here to inquire about your ghost," I said.

Darryl smiled, slightly surprised. "You want to know about Robert?"

"Who is Robert?"

Darryl described a doll. I thought I had hit a dead end until he told me about the doll's behavior. At this point, I figured Darryl was touched.

"Would you like to see the attic room where he lived?"

As he said this, a phone receiver flew off the hook toward me and stretched as far as the cord would allow before shooting back toward its original position and landing on the floor. Darryl shrugged it off as though this was a normal, everyday occurrence.

"I guess we should go."

We went to the second floor, and he led me up the staircase at the rear of the house. At the top, we found a closed hatch door. Darryl pushed open the hatch, and we went inside.

The ceilings were low with beams of exposed wood. A few boxes were stacked to the right. To the left I saw a doorway that led to the larger section of the attic. In front of me was a table, a double bench and a rocking chair, all sized as if they were crafted for a child. It looked as if a tea party was about to begin.

"These were Robert's," he said.

The atmosphere of the room seemed to change. A hot flash traveled the length of my spine. I felt dizzy and a powerful heat energy filled my stomach and chest. I tried to be polite, but I felt that I was going to be sick if I didn't get out of that room. I thanked Darryl for his time and made a quick exit.

I was starting to believe.

Nearly two decades have passed since that day. During that time, I have spent hundreds of hours uncovering thousands of documents about Robert. I have studied anything and everything related to Robert the Doll: his legends, his origins, stories about the people who owned him. Although we can now answer many questions about Robert, we are left with even more to ask.

What follows is the most comprehensive and accurate compilation of materials pertaining to Robert the Doll ever released; many of the materials are published here for the first time. In the process of researching this book I have become convinced there is something more to Robert than filling and fabric. Many of the people who agreed to be interviewed about their experiences have asked that their real names not be used, and we have redacted names from the letters sent to Robert.

My advice to anyone picking up this book: suspend disbelief until you have read the stories and their origins, looked over the accompanying documents, considered some of the theories, and paid a visit to Robert at the Fort East Martello Museum.

You might leave the Museum thinking that Robert is just a fascinating artifact that spurred a fantastic legend. But you just might find yourself writing a letter to the museum asking a doll to remove a curse, knowing that Robert did it.

Happy Hauntings.

David Sloan

ROBERT THE DOLL

Special thanks to Cori Convertito Farrar, Michael Gieda, Sharon Wells, Tom Hambright & The Kearney family for providing unrestricted access to key documents and other important research elements.

And to Heather-May Potter
for sticking around when things got weird.

THE LEGEND OF ROBERT THE DOLL

"Chucky isn't real.
Jason isn't real.
Freddy isn't real.
Robert the Doll... is real."

- Heather Clements

LEGEND:

A story handed down from the past; especially *one popularly regarded as historical although not verifiable.*

The legend of Robert the Doll continues to evolve. This is not uncommon for stories in the Florida Keys, a place where oral histories are told over drinks, and fishermen boast daily about the one that got away.

The good news is that some of these stories provide starting points for research, and many of the stories turn out to be based on fact. The bad news is that a lot of misinformation is passed on. Also, people tend to gravitate to the sensational, adding their own enhanced elements with each telling.

Such is the case with Robert the Doll. Robert was not the inspiration for Chucky in the *Child's Play* movies: Robert's hair is not human and he never jumped into the ocean after setting himself on fire while attempting to burn down a church.

But don't assume that the entire legend is false, just because Robert didn't inspire Chucky. Key West is the kind of place where fact is sometimes more disturbing than fiction, and the facts you are about to discover may keep you awake at night wondering if that noise under your bed is the house settling, or if Robert did it.

But first, the legend. It usually goes something like this:

Robert is a doll that was created around the turn of the century. He stands about three feet tall, is stuffed with straw, covered in felt, and dressed in a sailor suit. The doll has buttons for eyes, hair that continues to change in color as he ages, and a face that resembles a burn victim.

Robert was given as a gift to a young Key West boy named Gene Otto, and the boy and doll became inseparable. Some say Robert was a gift of love from a servant who lived in the Otto home, but others believe he was given by an angry servant who had been mistreated by the Otto family and sought revenge with the gift of a doll cursed with Voodoo. A lesser-known story claims Gene's grandfather, Joseph Otto, purchased the doll from a man he met on a boat trip to the Dry Tortugas.

Gene and Robert were constant companions, playing together night and day. Gene even went so far as to give Robert his name. You see, Gene was born "Robert Eugene Otto," but he went by his middle name as soon as the doll came into his life. When Gene was growing up, his parents would hear two distinct voices coming from the playroom; but when they went to see who was there, they would find only Gene and the doll. They became concerned when they tried to scold Gene for some misbehavior. Gene would look innocently at them and declare, *"I didn't do it. Robert did it!"* Some stories say that the parents would wake in the middle of the night to screams and find Robert holding Gene down in his bed.

Gene eventually went to school in Paris to study art, and met his wife Anne, a concert pianist. When the two returned to Key West many years later, Anne was shocked to find her husband creating a special room for Robert in the attic of the house, outfitting it with scaled furniture just right for the doll. He also created different outfits for Robert, including the sailor suit and a pixie outfit. Once again, man and doll became inseparable.

Gene used to paint in the turret room of the Artist House because it provided him the best light. While he was painting, he would place Robert in the window of the turret. People coming by the house would swear that they had seen Robert get up and move from one window to the other, and stories about Robert soon circulated with the school children around town. It is said that in his later years, Gene could be cruel or abusive to Anne, but when he was confronted with the abuse, his response was the same as it had been when he was a child. "I didn't do it. Robert did it."

Gene passed away in 1974 and Anne moved to Boston where she died a few years later. She left the doll behind, and when she rented out the house, there was a clause in the lease that specified: "Robert must remain the sole occupant of the attic room." After Anne moved to Boston, more strange stories emerged about Robert. Two men who rented the house heard constant noises coming from the attic. When they went to investigate they found the doll sitting in a different position with its legs crossed or its arms propped up over a chair.

A plumber doing work in the house heard giggling coming from behind him. When he turned around, he found the doll had moved from one side of the room to another. Another man who rented the house claimed that the doll had locked him in the attic for over a week, and also claimed that the doll had given him yellow fever. A family that purchased the house after Anne's death had a ten-year-old daughter who befriended Robert, only to wake up with him sitting on her face as if trying to smother her. Thirty years later, she still swears the doll was trying to kill her. Her father locked Robert in a trunk in the attic where the doll remained for many years. Shortly after he locked Robert in the attic, the man died from carbon dioxide poisoning in his car, parked in front of the house.

Robert was eventually donated to the Fort East Martello Museum, but the staff was so terrified of him that they kept him locked in a back room, covered with a sheet. If people wanted to see Robert, they had to make appointments; and the staff would go out of their way to create excuses to be elsewhere during the visits, or would schedule the visits on their days off. Although Robert had been moved from his childhood home, reports of paranormal activity in the home continued. Phones would fly off the hook, the doors to bookcases and bedrooms would open on their own, and people would feel as if they were being watched while in the attic room, a sensation usually accompanied by a feeling of negative energy and a burning sensation. People who came by the house with local ghost tours reported seeing the window shade in the turret window where Robert once sat being pulled to the side as if someone was peering out. When the ghost tour organizers checked with the guest house, they were told that the room was empty most of the time. There were also issues outside the turret room, where a particular shutter refused to stay open. A manager went so far as to screw it into the exterior wall of the house, but hours later it was again closed tightly.

Back inside the house, guests started reporting a ghostly female presence. A woman in a wedding dress would be seen walking down the stairs. A female presence would sit at the foot of guests' beds, and a brilliant blue orb would be seen circling the exterior of the property, sometimes materializing into a beautiful woman who stood watching from the second floor balcony. The theory started to emerge that Robert's spirit was getting stronger and the ghost of Anne Otto had returned to protect the house and all of its occupants from any misdeeds the doll might attempt.

Eventually Robert was placed on display in the Fort East Martello Museum. Dozens of people were requesting to see him each week, so the museum reluctantly put him in a display case along with some other artifacts of a darker nature. Paranormal activity decreased at the Artist House, but things started going crazy at the museum. Doors would slam, lights would flicker or turn on and off on their own, and people would report problems taking photographs of the doll. Some problems were as simple as camera batteries being drained in the doll's presence, only to be fully charged when people left the museum. Other visitors would develop their film to find that every picture had turned out except the pictures of Robert. One visitor picked up his film to find only 24 images of Robert in different positions; none of the other pictures turned out. Robert's legend continued to grow.

In the late 1990s, Robert underwent some restoration that included cleaning his sailor suit and his feet. He was put back in his locked case, but the next morning an employee arrived at the museum to see footprints in the dust of the museum floor. She heard tapping, and on investigation, realized that the sound was coming from Robert's case. The case was locked, but Robert's freshly cleaned feet were covered in dust and the employee heard a slight giggle.

Many theories have been expressed in an effort to explain the activity surrounding Robert. Some people believe an evil spirit possesses the doll. Others believe Robert was created with Voodoo or a soul stone that contains an ancient spirit. Perhaps Robert is just an innocent, misunderstood boy trapped in a doll's body. In any case, stories about bizarre encounters with Robert emerge from the museum every day, almost as quickly as the letters to Robert arrive. It appears that people will continue to blame Robert for a long time to come.

Dear Robert......

Could someone please read this aloud to Robert...

RECEIVED

Hello Robert,

In early September of last year (2011) my family and I visited you and Key West for the holiday weekend. We heard stories of you and decided to pay our respects to you on our way out of town. We asked for your permission to take your picture and nothing strange happened, and although we didn't voice our doubts out loud, perhaps you could sense that we were not real believers in you and your powers. Well, it has been about 6-7 months since our visit and since then my life has been one nightmare after another.

Within a couple weeks of returning home it started with my kitten suddenly dying, my bank account being fraudulently used TWICE, losing a substantial amount of money, having my bird die, my son falling and fracturing his skull, the hotel we stayed at on vacation set on fire, lost my job and now on the verge of being laid off of my new job, being forced out of my home, and my husband and I have separated.

I had been debating on writing this letter for weeks, but I'm now at the point where I'm desperate. I truly believe in you and the powers you possess, and kindly ask that you remove anything negative surrounding me and my family and give us your blessings. I have also removed the pictures that I have taken of you from Facebook.

Thank you.

ANATOMY OF
A HAUNTED DOLL

Michael Gieda (right), Dr. Cori Convertito (center) and Julio Rodriguez (left) remove Robert from his case for his annual examination.

What makes Robert tick?

The question has been asked for decades with no definitive answer. Each year, a team from the Key West Art & Historical Society evaluates Robert. His condition is monitored and staff members from different fields of expertise record attributes and identifying marks to preserve a permanent record of the doll and his history. Michael Gieda and Dr. Cori Convertito evaluated Robert on September 12, 2012 from 12:30 pm–2:30 pm. The report that follows represents the findings of this evaluation.

Robert the Doll Evaluation

- September 12, 2012
- 12:30pm-2:10pm
- Conducted by:

  Dr. Cori Convertito

  Michael Gieda

  David L. Sloan

- East Martello Museum
- Key West, Florida

Dr. Cori Convertito evaluates Robert the Doll.

Height: 40.25 inches

Weight: 6 lbs.

Head Length: 8.5 inches

Head Width: 6.5 inches

Head Circumference: 20.5 inches

Chest Size: 20.75 inches

Waste Size: 27.4 inches

Right Arm: 17 inches from top of joint

Left Arm: 17 inches

Hands: 7 inches where fabric change to fingertips

Right Leg: 21 inches (from top of joint)

Left Leg: 21 inches (from top of joint)

Right Foot: Sole 5.5 inches length, 3 inches width

Left Foot: Sole 5.5 inches length, 3 inches width

Eyes: Black wood buttons – 0.6 inches

Nose: 1.6 inches

Mouth: 2.25 inches across, 1.2 inches top to bottom

Neck: 10.9 inches

Ears: 2.5 inches vertical, 1.5 inches wide. Right ear replaced, likely during 2004 restoration. Left ear looks original with repair stitching.

Robert weighs in at 6 pounds on September 12, 2012

Evaluation Condition Report:

Interior: Robert has visible wire supports about the width of a coat hanger in his hands. Additional wires in the leg/hip area are slightly thicker and it is suspected that wire supports run throughout the doll, though x-rays have not been conducted to confirm this. Fabric deterioration on his fingertips, portions of the legs, arms and torso reveal a thin, dark, tightly packed, spun or woven straw known as *wood wool* or *excelsior stuffing*.

Exterior: Much of Robert's body is covered in felt cloth with the concealed areas crafted from a lighter weight cotton fabric. Limbs are attached to the torso with the thicker wire mentioned above. Elastic bandages were added during an earlier restoration to Roberts's ankles, wrists and neck to provide additional support to his fragile limbs. Deterioration of the fabric is witnessed sporadically across his body, particularly on the felt.

Head:

Pigments: There is evidence of light red or pink pigment used to enhance Robert's facial features on the lips, cheeks and nostrils, a common practice with dolls at the turn of the century. Light black pigment is visible above the eyes as small brows. All pigments have faded with UV exposure and age.

Eyes: Robert's eyes are slightly sunken, secured from beneath, made of wood shoe buttons, and painted black.

Ears: Robert's right ear was replaced with an acceptable substitute at an unknown date, likely 2004. His original left ear

Michael Gieda examines stitching on Robert's ear

remains intact, but degradation of the fabric is evident where each ear connects to the head. The head is formed with the same materials as the body.

Nose/Mouth: Both the nose and lips protrude slightly. Subtle stitching is visible, running vertically from chin to mouth. Oval stitching creates a form for Robert's lips and nose. A 'T' pattern stems from the bridge of his nose, crossing both eyebrows and meeting additional stitching at the crown of his head. Pink pigment is visible on his lips, and pink below his nose indicates nostrils.

Hair: His hair has elements of blonde and brown. Either could be the original color; blonde hair may have darkened with age, or brown hair may have lightened after years of UV exposure. His hair is short in length. The hairline runs high on his forehead and above each ear. Stitching on the crown beneath the hair indicates the location where his head was stuffed. The hair is believed to be mohair.

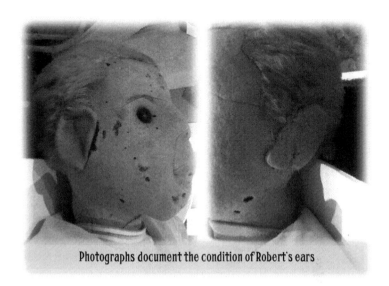

Photographs document the condition of Robert's ears

Clothing:

Robert wears a four-piece sailor suit consisting of pants, vest, jacket and hat.

Pants: The pants are of sailor style, white bell-bottoms with very slight yellowing from age. They contain 10 buttons ascending the thigh to the dolls center waist. Traditional Navy pants have 13 buttons. Slightly oversized, the pant legs are folded to a cuff above each foot. No markings were found on the pants to indicate origin.

Vest: The vest is decorative, covering only the front areas of the doll's chest not concealed by his jacket. It is white in color with a light blue *fouled anchor* embroidered on the upper chest and three stripes of light blue piping below the neckline. *Fouled anchor* refers to an anchor that has become hooked on the ground, or has its cable wound round the stock or

27

flukes. No markings or tags were observed on the vest to indicate origin.

Jacket: Robert wears a white sailor jacket with light blue and bright red markings. A single red band circles his right arm midway between shoulder and elbow, and a rating badge with a red eagle and anchor atop two red chevrons adorns the left arm in the same location.

According to http://navydads.com, Robert's rating indicates E-5 Petty Officer Second Class. The use of red usually indicates a naval fireman, but inconsistencies with traditional Navy code, as well as the size of the jacket, indicate it is not a Navy issued item. In addition to the ranking information, the jacket has two white buttons. The arm cuffs are light blue with two white stripes. The jumper flaps are light blue with three white stripes.

Of particular interest on the jacket is a label on the back collar that reads *"Best & Co., New York."* Albert Best founded Best & Co. as the Lilliputian Bazaar in 1879. The Lilliputian Bazaar initially focused on children's outfitting, but later included women's clothing and accessories. It was known for "tastefully styled and proper women's clothes and its sturdy children's wear." The flagship store was located near Sixth Avenue and 23rd Street in New York. A Best & Co. advertisement from 1901 offers a "Boy's Sailor's Blouse" much like the one Robert wears. According to Fort East Martello Museum's donation records, the sailor suit Robert wears originally belonged to Gene Otto.

Boy's Sailor Blouse

Of white lawn, white duck collar and sailor knot; collar, shield and cuffs trimmed with blue. **$1.00** Sizes 2½ to 8,

Many articles for special purposes, in addition to the greatest variety of everything usually kept for Children's wear, can be ordered by mail from our new Catalogue — sent for 4 cents postage.

Over 1000 Illustrations

WE HAVE NO AGENTS

Our goods sold only at this one store.

Address Dept. 1, 60-62 W. 23d St., N. Y.

A 1901 advertisement from the company who manufactured Robert's outfit for a boy's sailor blouse. (above) and the interior tag of Robert's hat (next page).

Hat: Robert's white sailor hat features a blue anchor with right facing eagle. An internal tag reads, *"Hat is made in the accordance with all material components and all manufacturing instructions required by U.S. Govt. and U.S. Navy specifications MH-H-47G (S.A.) Dated 22 October 1971. Size 7."* The label indicates the hat was not an original part of the doll's outfit. Elements of dolls' outfits are easily removed, and loss of some pieces is not uncommon.

Neckerchief & Sailor Knot: Best & Co. advertisements and naval tradition lead us to believe the outfit once included a black neckerchief.

Stuffed Animal: Robert holds a stuffed animal that resembles a lion, known to museum staff as *Leo*. The attached tag reads, "A.D. Sutton & Sons, New York City. Copyright 1964, Made in Japan." This would exclude the stuffed animal as an early companion of Robert but leaves open the possibility that the lion was with Robert during Eugene's lifetime. Reports from the donor indicate that the lion belonged to Eugene.

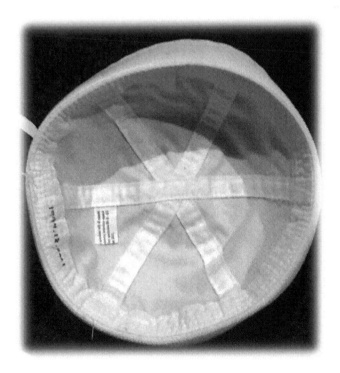

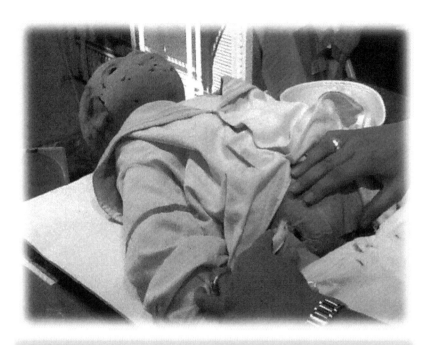

Above: a rare look beneath Robert's iconic sailor suit.

Robert's companion, Leo the Lion, and his identifying marks are documented below.

CONDITION AND CONSERVATION RECORD

PRIORITY : II

ACCESSION # ~~1994~~ 1994.18.0001   LOCATION OF #

NAME/TITLE Doll "Robert" w/ lion · chair

CIRCA: 1900
ORIGINAL DONATION DATE: 8·19·94

COMPOSITION:
Doll: Straw ; Felt ; wooden button eyes ; fur hair ; cotton muslin
metal wire
Clothes : Cotton
Chair: wood

DESCRIPTION :

Doll- stuffed w/straw: Head feet cover w/ fur hair and 2 wood buttons for eyes. Remnants of red coloring for nose and mouth. Various sm. holes in felt ®ear missing . © ear torn almost off

Head attached to body w/ metal wire . Body stuffed into muslin . Pink & green felt clothing in harlequin design

Hands w/ all fingers separate
Felt torn in numerous areas . Feet of brown felt

Sailor outfit - top and jacket and pants of white cloth w blue stripe at cuffs and collar. White bib & blue and/or embroidered
Hat not period
dated 1971   red embroidered and/or on © sleeve. Faded colors

Lion doll - gold velvet and fake fur w/ felt eyes. Dated 1964- not original

Chair - wood childs chair

32

Dear Robert...

Dear Robert,

RECEIVED

I have never met you in person before, but I have been researching you and at first did not believe in you. Then I made fun of you to my friend and then believed and gained the highest respect for you.

Since I made fun of you, I have accidentally broken an extremely valuable family heirloom and I am always really close to breaking things. I keep thinking that you're going to begin haunting me and I keep expecting to see you right in front of me. And to be honest, it scares me.

My dog keeps barking strangely... Can't animals sense spirits?

I just wanted to say I'm so sorry. I find you absolutely fascinating and I am definitely coming to visit you. I could bring you a present if you wanted. I'd like to take your picture, but I'm going to ask your permission first and apologize to you in person.

If the curse is on me, please lift it. I don't want to break any more things and that heirloom was really old. My mum was really upset!

Thank you.

MEET THE OTTOS

Robert 'The Doll' Otto

Robert the Doll arrived at 534 Eaton Street in Key West around the turn of the century and resided there until 1980. From 1980 until 1994, he lived at 1722-A Von Phister Street in Key West. On August 19, 1994, he was donated to the Fort East Martello Museum at 3501 South Roosevelt Boulevard in Key West where he remains on display today.

The unusual claims surrounding Robert are just a small part of his story. To gain a greater understanding, we need to look at the people who played a part in his development, influenced his history, and paved the path for Robert being where he is today. The most significant early influences in the life of the doll came from the Otto family.

Robert Eugene Otto

Robert Eugene Otto is best known for his role as Robert the Doll's lifelong companion. Born on October 25, 1900, "Gene," as he liked to be called, was a third generation native of the island and the youngest of four children; Mizpah (b.1892), Joseph (b. 1895) and Thomas Osgood (b. 1897). Gene was born in the family home at 534 Eaton Street that would one day be named the Artist House in his honor. The Otto family originally hailed from Prussia (now Germany), and Gene's father and grandfather both engaged in the practice of medicine.

The Key West where Gene Otto grew up was a true island with no bridges connecting it to the mainland. The Spanish American war ended just two years before his birth, the wrecking industry was starting to fade away, cigar manufacturing was the island's main industry, and a glass of lemonade cost just 20 cents. Beers were a quarter. Gene witnessed the hurricanes of 1906, 1909, and 1910 and was 11 years old when Flagler's first train arrived in Key West. The Ottos were by no means the richest family on the island, as some stories claim, Nevertheless, the family was well-off prior to the death of Thomas Otto, as shown by the family home built just before Gene's birth, and the two drug stores owned and operated by his father.

Doctors at that time did not make as much money as they do now, largely because they would treat patients regardless of ability to pay. For this reason, many doctors doubled as druggists, making most of their income on the pharmacy side of things. One of the Otto drug stores was located across the street from the family home on Eaton Street, and offered a variety of sundries as well as art supplies. This is likely where Gene acquired his first brushes and paints, starting a hobby that would lead to his later career. Family journals say he was painting before he could talk.

Some accounts of Gene's early relationship with the doll attempt to vilify the boy or give the appearance that something was wrong with him from an early age, but there is no evidence to back this up. At the turn of the century, there was not much of a stigma attached to boys having dolls. In fact, dolls of Robert's caliber were quite rare and would have

Give Watermelon Party.

A watermelon party was given last night by Misses Florence and Lillie Crittenton. Their guests were Misses Mildred Craft, Dorothy Albury, Elizabeth Lowe, Philis Rahner and Margaret Curtis; Messrs. Eugene Otto, Babcock Navarro, Will Norman, Kermit Light, Knight Johnson, Edward Lowe, Charles Lund, George and Nelson Crittenton.

been the subject of fascination. The teddy bear had only appeared on the scene around 1902, and children entertained themselves more with games than toys. As the youngest child, it is likely Gene was left to play alone while his older siblings were out; the doll would have made an ideal companion for him. Gene's wife would later claim the doll was Gene's best friend growing up because he didn't have any real friends—a fitting statement for the boy who would grow up to become an eccentric artist.

In September of 1921, Gene boarded a Mallory Steamer to attend the University of Virginia where he studied architecture for the next two and a half years. Robert was left at the family home. Determined to devote all of his efforts to the realm of painting, Gene then went to the Academy of Fine Arts in Chicago where he studied for three years. After this, he spent two and a half years at the Art Students League of New York working with the instructors there. From New York he moved to Paris where he established himself in a studio and met Annette Parker, his future wife.

T. Osgood Otto and Eugene Otto will shortly leave for the University of Virginia, the former to study medicine. while the latter will take up architecture. Osgood will leave September 4. going direct by rail, while Eugene will leave on the 6th, going by Mallory steamer via New York.

A September 1921 Miami Herald notice of Gene & Thomas Otto's college plans.

Annette Parker Otto

THE
GARLAND SCHOOL
OF HOMEMAKING

BOSTON, MASSACHUSETTS

Annette Parker is best known as the wife of Key West artist Gene Otto, but a look into her past reveals a dedicated, passionate and charismatic woman of many talents.

Anne, as she called herself, was born on December 9, 1902 in Cincinnati, Ohio to Gerard and Fannie Parker and spent most of her early years in New England. Anne came from a wealthy family who raised her in the Back Bay section of Boston, an area known for its brownstone homes. The older of two children, she had a close relationship with her younger sister, Lester.

Anne started studying piano at the age of five and then specialized in the instrument at the

39

National Cathedral in Washington D.C. In a 1939 interview with the *Daily Republican* she talks of interrupting lessons for her "bow to society;" a reference to her attendance at the Garland School of Homemaking. The Garland School was a finishing school of sorts, advertising itself as "a special school, which qualifies girls to preside over and maintain well-ordered homes." The school offered one-year and two-year homemaking courses including Child Study, Family and Social Problems, Food and its Preparation, Income and Cost of Living, Furnishings, Serving of Meals, and Handwork for Children. It was basically a school that taught Anne to be a perfect housewife; the school appears to have played a defining role in a life divided between her passion for music and dedication to her role in society. Upon completing her studies, she moved to Europe to once again pursue music. It was here she met her future husband, Gene Otto.

THE

Garland School

of Homemaking

A special school which qualifies girls to preside over and maintain well-ordered homes. One-and two-year homemaking courses under specialist teachers include Child Study, the Family and Social Problems, Food and its Preparation, Income and Cost of Living, Furnishings, Clothing, Serving of Meals, Stories and Hand Work for Children and many other vital home subjects. Also shorter elective courses. Resident students direct the Home-Houses (city and suburban) under supervision, putting into practice principles taught. Catalog on request. Address

Mrs. MARGARET J. STANNARD, Director
2 Chestnut Street, Boston, Mass.

Thomas Osgood Otto
&
Minnie Elizabeth Otto

Thomas and Minnie Otto hold the distinction of being the parents of Gene Otto and the first residents of the home where Robert the Doll spent his early years.

Thomas Osgood Otto was born in Key West on January 11, 1865. The son of Dr. Joseph and Maria Otto, he continued in his father's field of medicine but expanded the family practice with drug stores as his primary business. Thomas died on March 29, 1917, when Gene was just 16 years old. His obituary described him as one of Key West's noblest citizens whose upright and honest business dealings made him popular among men of all classes.

Thomas's wife, Minnie, was born Minnie Elizabeth Watkins in the Bahamas on March 28th,

1868. A white Bahamian, Minnie came to Key West with her family around 1872, according to the 1900 Census. The 1900 census shows the Otto family living at 412 Frances Street, with three children. Gene was born later that year in the new home at 534 Eaton Street. Both Minnie's birthplace and Thomas's line of business lend clues to the sources of stories surrounding Robert the Doll's origins, which will be discussed in a later chapter.

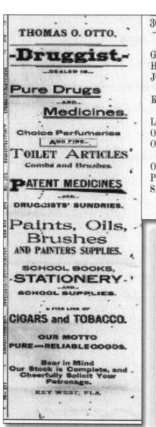

THOMAS O. OTTO.

-Druggist.-

...DEALER IN...

Pure Drugs
...AND...
Medicines.

Choice Perfumeries
AND FINE.
TOILET ARTICLES
Combs and Brushes.

PATENT MEDICINES
...AND...
DRUGGISTS' SUNDRIES.

Paints, Oils,
Brushes
AND PAINTERS SUPPLIES.

SCHOOL BOOKS.
-STATIONERY-
...AND...
SCHOOL SUPPLIES.

A FINE LINE OF
CIGARS and TOBACCO.

OUR MOTTO
PURE—RELIABLE GOODS.

Bear in Mind
Our Stock is Complete, and
Cheerfully Solicit Your
Patronage.

KEY WEST, FLA.

304   R. L. POLK & CO.'S KEY WEST DIRECTORY.

DRUGGISTS — Continued
Guichard Ysabel, 419 Duval
Hernandez & Co, 1005 Division
JOHNSON'S CHAS S DRUG STORE, 109 Duval
   (See right center lines)
KEY WEST DRUG CO, Simonton cor Fleming
   (See right center lines)
Lopez F J, 330 Southard
Oriental Drug Store, 536 Division
Otto T O, Eaton n w cor Simonton and Margaret
   cor Fleming
Owl Drug Co, 731 Whitehead
Paine F E, Division cor White
SAN CARLOS PHARMACY, 1101 Duval (See adv
   page 248)
   DRY GOODS AND NOTIONS.

The ad to the left shows items for sale at Dr. Thomas Otto's drug store including paints. oils. brushes and painters supplies. This may be where Gene Otto first discovered his passion for art. The ad appeared in *The Key West Druggist* a publication of Thomas Otto.

Above is a segment of the Key West Directory showing the locations of the Otto drug stores. one across the street from the family residence on Eaton and the second on the corner of Margaret and Fleming Streets where a health food store is now located.

Dr. Joseph Otto
&
Maria Belton Otto

There would likely be no Robert the Doll in Key West were it not for Gene's grandfather, Dr. Joseph Otto. Although he is not the doll's creator, his ancestral roots and the company he kept influenced events that would lead to Robert's arrival.

Accoriding to an Otto family history researched by Mizpah Otto, Dr. Otto was born in Konigsberg, East Prussia (Germany) on July 10, 1826, of noble lineage that can be traced back to Otto the Great of Prussia. He left his homeland during a student revolution, escaping to London in a load of hay. It was here that he assisted a 12-year-old girl who was stuck hanging on a picket fence by her petticoat. Six years later, Maria Elizabeth Benton became the doctor's wife.

Otto began his practice of medicine in Key West in 1862. He dealt with the smallpox and yellow fever epidemics, spending time at the Dry Tortugas, Indian Key, and Key Biscayne. His third son, Thomas Osgood, was born on the Coast Artillery Corps post and would grow to practice medicine like his father. Joseph would go on to be the first physician in the state to produce three generations of doctors.

The medical profession proved lucrative for the Ottos. Dr. Joseph's home was a three-storied mansion on Duval Street near Front St. with "the most magnificent royal Poinciana tree on the island" in his garden. Key West at the time was described as "an island known for its spacious homes and charmed gardens, its gracious hospitality and fine china and silver service." Otto served as City Health Officer and a vestryman at St. Paul's Church. He was beloved by the community and a distinguished, familiar sight on the streets as he made house calls to his patients.

In his later years, Otto became blind and was assisted in his duties by his servant, William Abbott. Although there are only a few mentions of William Abbot in the family archives, he apparently cared deeply for Dr. Otto. The Otto family's relationship with William Abbott and his wife Emeline is a probable source of the many servant legends surrounding Robert the Doll.

One afternoon while walking with William, Dr. Otto lost his footing and wrenched his body. The accident led to abdominal pain, and ultimately death. Otto died on June 27, 1885. He was 59 years old.

Mizpah Otto de Boe

Born in 1892, Mizpah Otto was the eldest of Thomas and Minnie Otto's children and the sister of Robert the Doll's constant companion, Gene Otto. Despite their 8-year age difference, Gene and Mizpah appear to have had a close bond throughout their lives.

Mizpah is responsible for much of the recorded Otto family history that appears in this book. Of particular value are her published histories of the Ottos who emigrated from Prussia and her hundreds of letters to her brother, Eugene, and his wife, Anne during their years in Paris, France.

The bond between Mizpah and Gene would prove detrimental to Anne after Gene's death, making Mizpah's role in the bizarre story of Robert the Doll even more significant. Mizpah probably knew more about the doll than anyone apart from Gene, but those secrets were taken with her to the grave in 1979.

Dear Robert...

Dear Robert,

I'm not totally sure if I personally did anything to upset you, but I'm sorry anyways. I'm pretty sure my dad didn't ask you for permission when he took a photo of you. For that I am also sorry. All I know is that very soon after seeing you in Key West and then returning home, my boyfriend of 10 months broke up with me and my dog got a cancerous tumor that they had to remove his whole tail to get off of him. I have also been diagnosed with depression and now my ex-boyfriend keeps insulting and being mean to me for no real reason.

Robert, if this is your doing, please reverse this curse. I want my old life back. I'm so sorry. I always thought you were cool and even bought a doll that looks like you because I though you're awesome. I'm sorry for whatever me or my dad did. Just please, please, please make it stop. I'm very, very, very, very sorry and I promise not to do it again.

With love,

████████

P.S. Did I mention how sorry I am and how cool you are? Because I am sorry and you are cool.

ROBERT'S FIRST HOME

PHOTO: NICK DOLL

Inside The Artist House...

One can only imagine the stories the Artist House would tell if her walls could speak. Home to two generations of Ottos, the residence of Robert the Doll for more than 70 years, and the most photographed home in Key West apart from Hemingway's former residence, the home-turned-guesthouse at 534 Eaton Street has hosted thousands of visitors through the years, sharing her history and enchantment with each of them along the way

Construction of the home started in the 1890s. A comparison of census records and family archives indicates that the Ottos moved to their new residence between June and October of 1900. The youngest Otto, Gene, was born in the home's second floor bedroom at the rear of the house. The Artist House has been described as "Key West —West Indian—Colonial—Victorian," a mish mash that makes it uniquely Conch and has earned the turreted home a place on all types of city tours. Much of the home's added features can be credited to Gene Otto himself, whose passion for art and architecture and incredible attention to detail drove him to make the house a true showpiece. One exception: the lavender shutters for which the house is known were not installed by Gene. Gene loved hues of green and continued the theme inside and out, even driving a green station wagon.

The interior of the home is warm and welcoming with modern conveniences and designs that complement the history evident in the 12-foot ceilings and ornate architecture. The guesthouse has seven rooms: the Sun Room, the Garden Room, the Morning Room, the Parlor Suite, the Eugene Studio Suite, the Anne Suite, and the Turret Suite. Upon entering the house, the visitor can easily imagine how the Ottos lived.

A hallway runs the length of the first floor with the staircase close to the entrance. The Parlor Suite is to the left; this suite served as the Otto family's parlor or living room. It was here that Anne's piano was played and guests were entertained. Pocket doors created intimacy or could be opened to the adjoining library, now known as the Garden Room. The third room on the first level was Gene's studio. The dining area adjoined his studio and the hallway.

 At some point, a butler's pantry was added. The pantry connected the dining room to the kitchen, which was originally a separate cookhouse. In the backyard, the Otto's cistern has been converted to a swimming pool but the statue of Saint Fiacre remains.

The second floor of the home has three main rooms; a fourth room, the Sun Room, has a private entry from the back garden stairs. Anne and Gene had separate rooms: Anne's suite at the back of the house and Gene's next to hers, now known as the Morning Room. The Turret Suite is found at the front of the house. The Turret Suite is significant for its magnificent turret, but also because this is the location where people claimed to see Robert the Doll moving from window to window on his own. The actual turret is on the third floor and only accessible through the second floor suite.

The living arrangements of Thomas Otto and his family are not known, but in piecing together the information available, it appears the turret room was a playroom for all of the children. The older siblings probably shared the Turret Suite below, leaving young Gene and Robert in the Morning Room close to Gene's parents, who shared Anne's Suite.

It should be noted that the Turret Suite is not the room Gene furnished as Robert's playroom. That room is in the attic above Anne's Suite, accessible by a narrow staircase.

Robert's domain: Stairs at the rear of the Artist House on the second floor lead to the attic room that Robert the Doll used to occupy. Today it is used as a storage area, but houses an effigy of the doll.

The Otto Residence: These photographs of the Otto home at 534 Eaton Street were taken in the 1950s when Gene and Anne Otto occupied the property with Robert.

The Otto Home today. Guests can now walk in the footsteps of the Otto family at the popular bed & breakfast known as The Artist House.
(Photos compliments of Nick Doll)

Dear Robert...

Dear Staff,

On August 10th we visited your fine museum. My daughter, my sister-in-law and I enjoyed our tour very much, and were impressed by the chatty and friendly woman at the desk. Despite the oppressive heat, we had a good time.

I was thoroughly acquainted with the legend surrounding Robert the Doll, and we were all very respectful to (and somewhat intimidated by) him. I asked Robert – aloud – if I could snap his picture. No one else was in the picture, and I felt it was ok. I don't think Robert agreed.

Since our visit to the museum, we've been under a dark cloud.

I began to develop a rather severe toothache. Two days later, Hurricane Charley cut our vacation short and we joined the parade of evacuees leaving the islands. We were evacuated from our vacation spot 3 days early with my mouth in tremendous pain. My sister-in-law was also having female health issues. We were all forced to make alternate travel arrangements on the run.

My sister-in-law lives in Clearwater. After a problem laden and horrendous trip, she finally got home, only to be evacuated from there too. She packed up her 2 cats and headed to her parents house in Winter Haven and wound up in the middle of the storm there. They lost power for two days.

(Letter continued on next page)

When we arrived in Miami for our flight back to Indianapolis, the plane broke and they had to "find" a different one for us. The following day, back in Indiana, I went to the dentist to learn that my tooth had abscessed and I had to have a root canal.

Last night we had a HUGE thunderstorm. Our house was hit by lightning, not once – but TWICE! We were unplugging things, but not fast enough. We lost 3 TV's and a large satellite dish. The first hit, which sounded like a gunshot in the house, took one large TV and the satellite dish, and the second hit got 2 more TV's. Again, the sound was horribly frightening.

Please do me a favor and tell Robert that we did not intend to anger or offend him and we're sorry if we did. His photo did turn out good, so he sat very nicely for me. Would he like it back?

Yours sincerely

Tales From The Turret

Here comes the bride...

Dozens of Artist House guests have reported seeing the ghostly figure of a woman in a wedding dress roaming the property. Eileene Chadwick stayed at the guesthouse in 1996 and was greeted almost immediately.

"My husband and I were staying in Anne's Suite. I unpacked my suitcase and was putting some things in the bathroom; I put my hair dryer in the sink and it immediately popped out and landed on the floor. I put it back in the sink and the same thing happened again. Moments later a beautiful woman dressed in white appeared. She walked through me and through the door. She had a playful look about her. I think she was curious about my hair dryer."

Other guests have reported seeing a woman in a wedding gown descending the staircase or watching the street from the second floor balcony. Most believe that the woman is Anne's ghost.

Poochie Myers says, *"In the big back bedroom on the second floor, there's a feminine presence, a very warm, loving energy. That was Anne Otto's room and her loving energy is still there."*

Apparitions wearing wedding dresses are not uncommon. Weddings are important dates marked with a great deal of energy and emotion, so it is not out of the question for spirits to return in ways that reflect them at their happiest. Gene's mother Minnie and his sister Mizpah were also brides who called 534 Eaton Street home, but the humor, beauty, and poise people associate with the ghost's appearance are more characteristic of Anne.

Another factor to consider is the translucent quality of many apparitions, which might give any period dress the appearance of a wedding gown and lead to sightings of "brides."

ORIGINS:
A DOLL IS BORN

Robert's creation has generally been pegged to have taken place in the first five years of the 20th century, with 1904 being the most common year referenced. The most pressing question was never when he was created but rather – who created him?

Most theories of Robert's origin involve slighted servants and Voodoo. Although both of these likely played a role in the story of the doll, his true origin—although not quite as sinister—is equally fascinating. If you suffer from coulrophobia (fear of clowns), now is the time to pick up a different book.

Robert is a clown who was crafted in Germany.

In 1880, German entrepreneur and seamstress Margarete Steiff, who was confined to a wheelchair, began making felt elephant pin cushions from a pattern published in a women's magazine called *Modenwelt.* Noticing that children enjoyed playing with them, Margarete went on to design and create other popular animal-themed toys. A few years later, with the assistance of her brother Fritz, she formed the Steiff Company. Today, over a century and a quarter later Steiff is still universally recognized for its quality, workmanship, and fantastic designs.

Although best known for their 1902 invention of the teddy bear, the Steiff Company can also take credit for the creation of Robert the Doll.

The final touch on any Steiff toy is its trademark "button in ear" devised by Margarete's nephew Franz in 1904 to prevent counterfeits from being passed off as authentic Steiff toys. The button is metal and originally had the symbol of an elephant, later replaced by the name "Steiff." The fact that Robert the Doll was missing the right ear that would have contained the Steiff trademark—the ear having likely been pulled off by Gene as a child—left Robert's origins open to speculation for nearly 50 years.

Robert's factory of birth in Giengen is pictured below. Above are some employees of the Steiff Company at a 1903 Christmas party. It is very possible that several people in this photo helped create Robert.

One of today's leading experts on everything Steiff is Steiff's Consultant and Archivist for North America, Rebekah Kaufman. Suspecting that Robert was a Steiff creation, I contacted Rebekah through mysteifflife.blogspot.com. After we exchanged detailed photos, descriptions and measurements, Rebekah was fairly certain that Robert was an authentic Steiff manufactured prior to 1912. A German colleague of Kaufman agreed, but 100% certainty for identification of such a rare doll is difficult to achieve with photos alone.

The following year, Rebekah discovered a very similar doll, most definitely Steiff, up for auction. This pretty much answered the questions about Robert's origins.

Despite being made by a well-known company, Robert remains extremely rare and perhaps one of a kind, even without factoring in the paranormal aspects associated with him. Given his impressive size, Kaufman believes he might have been intended as a window display or "studio style" item, meaning he was manufactured on the scale of a real person. She also noted that Robert would have been a very expensive item at the time, so only a person of affluence (or a person who was associated with affluence) would have been able to afford the doll.

But how did Robert come to travel from Germany to Key West? Rebekah suggested searching for a German connection. It was not hard to find.

Gene's grandfather, Dr. Joseph Otto, is the obvious connection to Germany, having hailed from Prussia. Some legends claim Joseph acquired Robert for his grandson while on a boat returning from the Dry Tortugas, although his death in 1885 makes this chronologically impossible.

A family history prepared by Gene's sister, Mizpah, notes that Joseph maintained good communication with his kin in Germany through the years. There is also evidence that gifts were exchanged between the German and American Ottos.

This, along with other evidence, leads us to believe that Gene's mother may have brought Robert to the United States on a return trip from Hamburg.

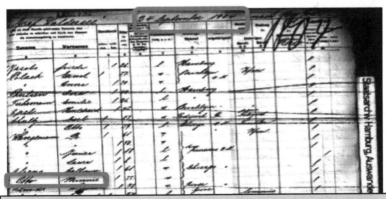

A passenger list for the Hamburg-Amerika Line's *Graf Waldersee* shows Minnie Otto returning from the Otto's homeland on September 24, 1904. This supports the 1904 creation date attributed to Robert and would place the doll in Key West just before Gene's birthday.

The new information leaves one glaring question: What about the story of the angry servant who gave the doll to Gene?

It should be noted that Gene's mother, Minnie Otto, came from the Bahamas. Minnie was white Bahamian, but the stories about Robert show him variously as a gift from a Bahamian woman, a gift from a black girl, a gift from a servant, and a doll crafted with Voodoo by a mistreated slave.

Most stories passed down through the verbal tradition suffer a similar fate, changing with each repetition. In the case of Robert, however, there is some evidence of an angry servant who was close to the family and may have used Voodoo on the doll after it was created.

Robert embarked on his journey to the United States dressed in a pink and green Harlequin clown suit adorned with pom-poms. This was the outfit he wore the day he met little Eugene for the first time.

Robert's transportation? The Hamburg-Amerika Line's *Graf Waldersee* brought Minnie Otto back from Germany in Sept. 1904.

65

The rare Steiff doll pictured above shows a Harlequin clown costume similar to the one Robert was wearing when first created. The iconic sailor suit Robert wears now belonged to young Gene Otto and became one of the doll's many uniforms.

Dear Robert...

RECEIVED

Dear East Martello,

Last month my boyfriend and I visited East Martello. I was especially interested in Robert the Doll. Mark made several comments about all the hype and hysteria about Robert. He insisted it was just a ruse to get people in the door at the museum and made a number of rude comments about Robert. I am far more inclined to believe the stories, and now so is Mark.

As soon as we left the museum things started to go wrong for Mark. At 31 years old he received his first speeding ticket, just around the curve from the fort. Next we missed our flight back to Chicago. When we finally did get back home, my bags arrived without incident. However, Mark's bags were lost for nearly two weeks! Unfortunately, Mark's diabetic supplies were all in his luggage, so he had to replace all of them.

When we arrived home, our dog, who is very friendly and has NEVER shown any signs of hostility, began to attack Mark: growling, snarling, and going for his ankles and throat. It took almost two weeks - about the same time it took his bags to arrive, before the dog returned to his regular demeanor. It was never directed toward anyone except Mark.

All of my vacation photos came out beautifully, but all of Mark's were ruined except the ones in the camera, and those were all of Robert. My sister plans to visit and hopes to smooth things out for Mark.

67

BOY MEETS DOLL

An early photograph of Minnie Otto and her 4 children. From left:
Thomas Osgood. Joseph. Eugene and Mizpah.

The relationship formed between Eugene and
his doll was far from normal by most accounts.
Stories from those familiar with Gene and Anne vary
only slightly. William Reuter, Myrtle Reuter and
Nancy Tazwell each owned the Artist House at some
point after the Ottos sold the house. Each was
familiar with Robert, and all knew Gene and Anne in
their later years. They shared their insights in an
early 1990s interview with Arthur Myer:

"Gene had a doll that people said was haunted. It was made as an effigy of him when he was a five-year-old boy. It was his doll. It was supposed to have some magical property. A lot of people feel that way about it."

—William Reuter, Owner of Robert and the Artist House, 1974–1980

"The story I heard was that Gene Otto had a doll when he was a little boy that was his mirror image. It was supposedly made to look like Gene. It wore the same clothes. I've seen it. It had several outfits, supposedly the same outfits that Gene had when he was a little boy. All the bad things that Gene did were blamed on the doll, so that the doll took on all the kind of negative karma of Gene as he was growing up. He was a bad doll. Later on when things happened in the house it was supposedly the spirit of the doll. Gene would always say he hadn't done it—the doll had done it. Everything that was negative was put onto the doll."

—Nancy Tazwell

"It's a large doll, as big as a child. I don't know if it was made in the image of Gene because I never knew him as a child. It has hair on it like a real child. It has buttons for eyes. It has different kinds of clothes. It was in a pixie outfit when I got it. People around Key West don't like the doll."

—Myrtle Reuter, Robert's caretaker from 1974–1994

A 1985 article that ran in *The Sun Sentinel* backs up the claim:

> *"It is about the size of a six-year-old child, and dressed in a pink and green Harlequin costume. Its face is round, the hair blonde and closely cropped, but with pinched features. Its eyes are blank beads. The overall effect is subtly unpleasant. Robert Eugene Otto loved the doll. He had loved it since he was a child, when it had been given to him by a black girl his parents had helped raise. Otto adopted the doll as his alter ego. He named it ``Robert," and when he would get in trouble he would blame the doll. ``Robert did it," he would say."*

—*Scott Eyman,* Sun Sentinel, 1985

Young Eugene Otto plays with an unknown companion while wearing the now iconic sailor suit sported by Robert the Doll.

Dear Robert...

RECEIVED

Dear Staff,

I was working for a local paper & was sent to the Martello Fort to photograph an event. I took various shots of the outside sign, staff hosting the event, etc. as I was making my way through the front sections of the museum. I occasionally checked to see that the photos were metered right for lighting, etc. All was fine camera in working order; pictures, clear & fine.

I casually moved along & saw Robert. I figured I'd be polite & asked him if it was ok that I photograph him & the night's event. Not feeling any 'ill will', I took my shots and continued on my night.

When I got home & reviewed my work – the photos pre-Robert were all there, but the shots of him & the rest of the night no longer existed. GONE. I did nothing to my camera (changing lenses, or setting, battery was working, etc.) NOTHING WAS WRONG. I guess Robert was feeling naughty that night. Needless to say, I didn't have my work published for that event.

As a side note, I recently was back at the fort. I wanted a shot of Robert (maybe just for spite!) I waited until there were several people around him, distracting him. I got the photo & the rest of my pics were all fine too!

Sincerely

Tales From The Turret

Down on the drapes...

A number of people with varying degrees of sensitivity to the spirit world have stayed at the Artist House in hopes of communicating with the spirits. Most leave with little more than a relaxing stay, but several have claimed communication with different spirits at the inn.

Nancy Tazwell purchased the home from the Reuters in 1980 and felt that the energies were centered in the turret.

"It's my understanding that this was where the doll was kept. The cupola was Gene Otto's place in the house when he was a child and later on when it was his studio. When I would walk up the steps there would sometimes be like a cold wind, and the windows would shake as though there were a storm going on. I didn't find it frightening. I would say things like 'Don't worry, I am a friendly spirit.' I wish now I had been more aware. It seems that I was always so busy rushing around that I didn't take very much time to experience the sensations of the house."

A German couple stayed in the Turret Suite, and although the husband felt nothing, his wife claimed she felt a presence that grew stronger with every step up the room's staircase.

Perhaps the strangest report came in 1998 from a woman who claimed no psychic ability. She approached the front desk and told the manager, *"She doesn't like the new drapes."*

What makes the last story curious is the fact that the drapes had recently been changed. Interviews with those familiar with the Otto home during Gene and Anne's residence often cite the beautiful green and yellow drapes that adorned their windows.

Did Robert do it? Mizpah Otto and an unknown helper clean up a mess surrounding a chair identical to the one Robert now occupies at the Fort East Maretllo Museum. The photographer is also unknown.

SERVANTS & VOODOO

Tales of Voodoo and mistreated servants go hand in hand with the story of Robert the Doll. Although it has been proven that a mistreated servant or Voodoo practitioner did not create Robert, there is plenty of evidence that Voodoo played a role in Robert's development. At least one theory involving a mistreated servant may have been the source of the many legends involving servants and slaves with the doll.

William Abbott immigrated to Key West from the West Indies some time prior to 1880 with his wife Emeline. William was mulatto, Emeline black, and both had lineage traced to the Bahamas. William started as a laborer in Key West, Emeline a laundress. At some point, William became a servant to Dr. Joseph Otto, driving his buggy and attending to him when he became blind. One anecdote explaining Dr. Otto's attention to detail, despite his lack of vision, described the doctor running his hand over the sheet before getting into bed and saying, "William, there's a wrinkle in my sheet." Additional accounts of their relationship are scarce, but it appears they had a great admiration for each other.

William remained by Dr. Otto's side until his death in 1885, at which time Thomas Otto, Eugene's father, hired William as a clerk at the family pharmacy across the street from the Otto's Eaton Street home.

The years that follow leave more questions than answers. William continued to work for Gene's father until Joseph Otto died in 1916. The fact that he escorted Thomas Otto's brother to the West coast when Thomas' health was failing, then returned with the body after he passed, shows a closeness and trust between William and the entire Otto family. But what about William's wife, Emeline?

There is speculation that she may have been close too. Perhaps a little too close.

Although there is no single document yet discovered that comes right out and says "Thomas Otto had an affair with William Abbott's wife, Emeline, and she gave birth to his child," information obtained from several documents is cause for speculation.

- Minnie Otto's journals acknowledge that many women wished they were wed to her doctor husband. They resented Minnie because she didn't come from wealthy stock.
- Thomas Otto's father advised him "not abstinence, but prophylactic care" of his health against venereal diseases.
- Emeline Abbott gave birth to, and lost, a child sometime between 1900 and 1910.
- Emeline Abbott attempted to initiate a lawsuit against the Otto family shortly after Thomas Otto's death.
- Minnie Otto chose to be buried outside of the Otto family plot.

All of these documents are circumstantial at best. Consider also that a half dozen people have reported encountering the spirit that resides in Robert, and have described it as a mulatto or light-skinned black child. This leads to more questions:

- Is Robert the spirit of a deceased child born of William and Emeline Abbott? Or a child born of an affair between Thomas Otto and Emeline Abbott?
- Could this child be the 'black girl associated with the Otto family' mentioned in early newspaper articles?
- Did Emeline use Voodoo as a way to remain close to her only child by trapping its spirit in the doll?
- Was Eugene attached to the doll because it contained the spirit of his half brother or sister or a childhood playmate?

Poochie Myers took care of the Artist House for a period in the 1980s. A psychic sensitive, Poochie described the ghost of a little girl who sits on the staircase, scrunched up in a little white, old-fashioned nightgown. She describes her with long, light brown curls, about five years old and very angry about something. Could this be the same child?

We may never know, but it leaves Emeline and William Abbot as the likely inspiration for many of the stories surrounding Robert the Doll. And then there is the Voodoo. The following quotes came from interviews conducted by Arthur Myers.

INDIVIDUAL RECORD OF BURIAL — KEY WEST, FLORIDA

1. Abbott _____ LAST _____ ~~Ernestina~~ EMIMEILINE _____ FIRST _____ MIDDLE
2. ADDRESS ~~517 Pinder Lane~~ STREET _____ Key West CITY OR TOWN _____ Fla. STATE
3. GRAVE NO. _____ LOT NO. _____ BLOCK NO. _____ SECTION _____
4. OWNER OF LOT OR GRAVE SPACE _____ PURCHASED _____
5. DATE OF DEATH ~~July. 27, 1925~~ PLACE Key West, Fla.
6. CAUSE ~~High blood pressure~~ DATE OF BURIAL ~~July 29.; 1925~~
7. BURIAL RECORDED IN BOOK 17 _____ PAGE 630
8. SEX F COLOR B MARITAL STATUS W AGE 58 YRS.
9. DATE OF BIRTH X PLACE Bahamas
10. NEXT OF KIN _____ ADDRESS _____

---

from map

INDIVIDUAL RECORD OF BURIAL — KEY WEST, FLORIDA

1. Abbott _____ LAST _____ Wm _____ FIRST _____ MIDDLE
2. ADDRESS _____ STREET _____ CITY OR TOWN _____ STATE
3. GRAVE NO. A LOT NO. 182 BLOCK NO. Tract 6 SECTION 2nd Ave
4. OWNER OF LOT OR GRAVE SPACE J. Otto PURCHASED _____
5. DATE OF DEATH MAY 9, 1916 PLACE _____
6. CAUSE _____ DATE OF BURIAL MAY 10, 1916
7. BURIAL RECORDED IN BOOK _____ PAGE _____
8. SEX _____ COLOR _____ MARITAL STATUS _____ AGE _____
9. DATE OF BIRTH _____ PLACE _____
10. NEXT OF KIN _____ ADDRESS _____

Burial records from the Key West cemetery show Emeline and William Abbott interred in the Otto Family plot. A shared plot between blacks and whites at the time was rare and indicates an unusual intimacy between the two families. The Abbotts may be responsible for some of the voodoo claims attributed to Robert.

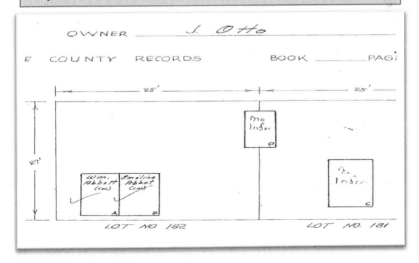

OWNER _____ J. Otto

E COUNTY RECORDS _____ BOOK _____ PAGE

25'   25'

27'

Wm. Abbott (cas) | Emeline Abbott (cgs)

LOT NO. 182   LOT NO. 181

77

"Everybody says it's Voodoo, but I've never had any trouble with the doll."

—*Myrtle Reuter, Robert's caretaker 1974-1994*

"A lot of Key Westers are very much into what is something of a combination of Voodoo and Catholicism. There's a Cuban influence, but it's practiced by people of all sorts. The doll that Gene Otto had was supposed to be something like his alter ego."

—*Tom Hambright, Monroe County Historian*

"You know, there is a strange religion down here like a sort of Voodoo. Eugene being an artist, I think he probably experimented with these things. Local people won't talk much about this, so I haven't gotten many answers."

—*Ed Cox, former owner of The Artist House*

"People around Key West don't like the doll. They believe in Voodoo, and they don't want to come in contact with it."

—*Myrtle Reuter, Robert's caretaker 1974-1994*

"We left a man who was studying to be a lawyer to live in the house while we were gone. He wrote this fantastic story that the doll was Voodoo and it locked him up in the attic and he caught yellow fever."

—*Myrtle Reuter, former Artist House owner*

"Some folks speculate that the doll has a crystal inside that collects negative energy and then returns it to the owner."

—*Darryl Meyer, former Artist House owner*

"Little beaded Voodoo figures that rested in Robert's lap would occasionally be found against the opposite wall, as if Robert had heaved them in a fit of temper."

—*Scott Eyman,* Sun Sentinel, *1985*

Santeria is the prevalent form of Voodoo practiced in the Florida Keys. The term is derived from a time when slaves disguised the African Orishas they worshiped with the identity of Catholic saints to avoid further persecution. Several theories suggest that Santeria is responsible for Robert's abilities - abilities that are not normally associated with dolls.

But whether it was Voodoo or a different force that created the bond between Gene Otto and Robert the Doll, Gene had responsibilities and obligations that didn't include Robert.

In June of 1918, Gene left the only home he had ever known to take up architecture at the University of Virginia. Soon after, he began pursuing his passion for art, spending three years at the Academy of Fine Arts in Chicago. This was followed by two years at the Art Students League of New York. Robert was not part of the plan, and remained in Key West.

As the years passed, it appears Robert waited patiently for his companion to return to 534 Eaton Street, but visits were limited to holidays and special occasions. In 1924, Gene moved to Paris where he studied the Expressionist European painters. He painted at la Grande Chaumière, Collorossi and Delecleuse Academy, augmenting his Paris work with trips into Italy and Spain.

Twenty-seven years would pass before the two would be together again.

Dear Robert...

Dear Robert,

I had the great pleasure of visiting Key West in 2005 I believe it was. The summer of Hurricane Dennis. That was the beginning of everything most horrible to come in my life.

I remember vividly the day we visited your museum, or rather, the museum you now reside in. My family and my love of 5 year's family were all there. We took pictures of you in your little case. I did ask if you minded, but I also had a faint disbelief at the time. That has all changed since. I remember the slight silliness I felt asking permission to take a dolls picture. I have wished many times since that I had not taken those pictures. Only moments after, the loud speakers announced that all tourists were ordered off the island because of Dennis! And my life has been an agonizing wheel of pain ever since.

The one love of my life walked out of my world only three months later. It took me three years to find this love and it devastated me. I nearly lost my mind. I have had scraps with the law, lost a very good job, have been isolated from family members. The list of horrors goes on and on. It has been one misfortune after another. Way too many to list.

Then finally about six months ago you crossed my mind and I have decided that so much misfortune in such a short time has to be from some kind of curse. So I am writing to you to ask

(letter continued on next page)

that you accept a heartfelt apology from me. I truly believe in things bigger than what meets the eye now. Cursed is how I believe I have been living my life ever since our encounter. I ask that you please extinguish your grip on my life so that I may find some peace. Never will I question the unknown with so much disregard again. I feel now that there are forces in the world not to be laughed at. I have been plagued with misfortune and pain but I have learned to question the impossible.

So I hope that you will see fit to accept my apology and this dark cloud will be lifted from my life.

Sincerely,

THE PARIS YEARS

Mizpah Otto joins her brother Eugene and his fiancée Annette Parker in the Paris flat the couple would occupy after their marriage.

"Les Annees Folles" (the mad years) describes the fascinating decade in France that began after the First World War and ended with the economic crash of 1929. Upper and middle classes replaced their pre-war values with aspirations for care-free debauchery which would lead to a cultural scene that swept literary, fashion, artistic, and musical circles across much of Europe. Hemingway, Fitzgerald, Picasso and Matisse brought their talents to the party, as did the artist Eugene Otto.

Paris was the place to be. It was here that Gene would develop his artistic style and meet the companion who would give Robert the Doll a run for his money. Gene's sister, Mizpah, described in her journal how her brother met his future wife:

"My beloved little artist brother has been studying art for three years in Paris at Academie Julienne, and working out his art's salvation alone. A year ago last February he was awakened by strains of exquisite music which floated up to him from a little salon below his. Leaning over his balcony, he listened while the young pianist played. Loitering on the stairways long and frequent enough, he met her to instantly love her."

It was a fairytale romance by most accounts. Annette Parker spent time between London and

Paris with Gene courting her every step of the way. Gene's mother, Minnie, traveled with her son to meet Annette in London. Gene made a special trip to Boston and asked Mrs. Parker for her daughter's hand. When it was Anne's time to leave Paris, Gene bombarded Mrs. Parker with pleading cables from across the Atlantic, until finally she agreed to allow her daughter to wed. With Anne's sister, Mrs. Parker boarded a steamer bound for Paris.

According to the society pages, Gene Otto searched all of Paris for a gift for his fiancée. He found nothing lovely enough to satisfy him until his eye caught the sparkle of a delicately wrought silver cross set with white sapphires. There was a problem: the cross was around a shopkeeper's neck and she assured him it was a treasured personal possession.

Gene pleaded, bribed, and nearly threatened the shopkeeper, but she remained unmoved until Gene blurted out that he wanted it for his fiancée. The shopkeeper then became his ally, and after chastising him for failing to tell her whom it was for, presented him the cross at no cost as her gift to Annette.

Miamian's Marriage In Paris of Interest To His Friends Here

Robert Eugene Otto and Miss Annette Parker of Brookline, Mass., Wed May 3.

Of social interest here where he has spent much of his time is the announcement of the marriage of Miss Annette Parker, daughter of Mrs. Gerard Lester Parker of Brookline, Mass., and Robert Eugene Otto of Paris and Miami, which took place May 3 in the American Cathedral in Paris.

The bride's mother was present as was her aunt, Mrs. William Howard Richardson of Cincinnati. Miss Lester Parker, a sister of the bride, was her attendant. The relatives left the United States in April to attend the wedding.

The bride is the granddaughter of an early governor of Massachusetts. Her family is prominently identified with the early history of the state. She specialized in piano at National Cathedral in Washington and later attended the Garland school in Boston. For a year and a half she has traveled and studied abroad, spending much time in London and Paris.

Mr. Otto, the son of Mrs. Thomas Osgood Otto of Key West, is widely known here where he is an associate member of the Aux Arts Decoratifs. He is a graduate of the University of Virginia. Mr. Otto has spent much time in Paris as a student of painting and buys for his firm here. He is a brother of Dr. Thomas Osgood Otto, James Otto and Mrs. Michael Price DeBow of Miami. Following a short wedding trip in southern France the couple will reside in Paris.

* * *

Annette Parker wed Eugene Otto at the American
Cathedral in Paris on May 3, 1930. Gene's mother said of Anne:
"God never made another like her. Her nature is music.
This romance is the kind one dreams of."

Several family members accompanied Annette and Eugene on their honeymoon through Italy. Robert the Doll remained in Key West.

Dear Robert...

Dear Robert.

I unwittingly took your picture on my phone without your permission. I thought that if you did not tip your head it meant yes, now I very clearly understand it meant no.

The evening I took it, I broke my tailbone and sprained my wrist on Duval Street and the next evening as I went to delete the photo out of my phone, a light in my hotel room that was turned off began to flicker.

Anyhow, I am very sorry. Please accept my apology and thanks for letting me meet you!

Please remove your curse.

P.S. – I put the wall piece back.

Tales From The Turret

The Séance...

A séance was held in the Turret Suite of the Artist House in 1997 in anticipation of Robert the Doll's television debut on a show called *Strange Universe*. Thirteen people were present, including Darryl Meyer who owned the home at the time, several employees of the Artist House, their friends, and two witches, Jay and Renee, who owned a metaphysical shop in Key West called The Wizard's Attic.

Guests toured the attic room before gathering in the lower portion of the Turret Suite to watch for Robert's appearance. When the tour was finished, candles were lit and the group gathered in a circle on the floor while Jay and Renee explained how the séance would work.

Jay was to lead the séance. Renee would put herself in a receptive trance so as to allow the spirit of Robert to speak through her. Members of the circle would be permitted to ask questions as contact was attempted.

Different rituals were performed with no results. Questions were asked with no perceptible responses. After 30 minutes, the only activity noted was a bizarre flare from one of the candles and the sound of an item being dropped on the floor, although no source of the sound could be found.

After 45 minutes, the séance ended with everyone disappointed by the results. But after the séance, one of the participants attempted to climb the stairs to the turret and was stopped by an unseen force. Jay joined him, and together they were able to ascend against great pressure, as if pushing against an inflated balloon. Upon reaching the top they witnessed surreal chaos as thousands of misshaped orbs fled the room through every window and wall.

Renee conversed in the room below. Suddenly she screamed for everyone to leave, and then broke down in tears. Jay believes the turret opened up as a "spirit waiting room," and felt the spirits were upset that it had been penetrated. Renee was shaken for days and claimed she had never felt a spirit force like the one that entered her that night. She believes it was Robert.

THE NEW YORK YEARS

Annette and Eugene moved to New York City in the mid-1930s, during the Great Depression. The Otto family money dried up after Gene's father died in 1916, although his mother did everything she could to conceal this fact. The Parker family took a Black Tuesday hit like many, but their superior financial situation left them with their heads further above water than most.

Art is one of the first luxury items people stop buying when the economy is depressed, so Gene took a job selling furniture in John Wannamaker's department store. Gene had an eye for antiques, and when he and Anne moved to New York, they brought an impressive collection of items acquired in Europe.

Anne arrived in the Big Apple with her musical talents and charm, which is all she ever seemed to need. One New Year's Eve the Ottos were entertaining guests in their apartment when it was suggested Anne should share her talents with the city. Anne rose to the challenge, promising that by the same time next year she would be performing at the next club mentioned on the radio. An advertisement for the prestigious Rainbow Room at Rockefeller Center came on. Several months later, Anne Otto was performing there under the pseudonym, Anne Gerard.

Music became the focal point of Anne and Gene's life in New York. Together they composed and copyrighted more than 30 songs where Gene wrote the lyrics and Anne provided the musical composition.

Their song *Of Time and The River* was recorded by Jimmy Brierly, but competition in the music business was tough, as Anne would recall in an interview for the society pages after relocating to Key West.

News that Gene's mother was ill came in 1945. Eugene was 45 years old, Annette, 43. Together they packed their belongings and embarked on a new adventure to Gene's hometown of Key West.

Anne would later regret leaving New York and her gig at the Rainbow Room, but her loyalty to her husband prevailed over any personal decisions.

Anne and Gene Otto made a home in this New York City building for nearly a decade before heading to Key West.

Meanwhile Anne Gerard is standing on the threshold of her career. Although known to society as an accomplished pianist, Anne has just made her professional swing debut at the Rainbow Room in Rockefeller Center in New York City.

The story really starts last New Year's Eve when Anne was playing for a group of friends. One of them suggested that she really ought to be playing in a night club where more people could hear her.

Anne agreed thoughtfully. Then with a sudden change of mood she snapped on the radio and announced that the next night club named would be her place of business on the following New Year's Eve. The other waves answered her with the Rainbow Room. And Anne laughingly says now that she doesn't know whether she would have done it if it had been the Cotton Club.

What she did do, however, was to go to New York and find a friend who knew a friend who knew a friend — who got her an audition at the Rainbow Room. And now

"Our honeymoon was spent on the French Riviera," Mrs. Otto said. "It was surprising how far a few American dollars went in France in those days."

Europe was the Otto's home until the mid-1930s when the U.S. went off the gold standard. "That's when we returned to the States, spending the next ten years in New York" she said.

While her husband continued painting, Mrs. Otto returned to her music as a professional pianist playing in night spots and New York supper clubs.

"A six-month engagement at the popular Rainbow Room still stands out in my memory as the highlight of my musical career," Mrs. Otto said. "So many exciting and amusing things happened there."

"Besides playing and painting, Gene and I collaborated in writing popular songs. He did the lyrics and I, the music. But it's a competitive business."

Two of the Ottos' songs were published but neither made the hit parade, she said.

An artist with an established reputation, Otto decided to return to his family's two-story, turreted old Coach house when his mother became ill in the 1940s.

His wife carefully packed up their 18th century copper collection and priceless antiques gathered in France and Italy and they headed for home.

In the living room there's a full-length portrait of Mrs. Otto painted by her husband. It wears a perpetual "No Sale," tag, for it's their favorite painting.

In Charge
Robert Eugene Otto
Formerly of
John Wanamaker's
New York

Winthrow Rockefeller heard the audition of a comely lady named Anne Gerard at the Rainbow Room several weeks ago and she stroked the keyboard of a piano so well that he signed her up. After a few days Miss Gerard's real identity was revealed to be Mrs. Eugene Otto, one of Boston's oldest social families. When this connection with the Cabots and Lodges came to light Miss Gerard was alarmed. "I guess," she said to the manager one night, "that you'll fire me now!" . ; .

Born in Boston of a Back Bay family, she started studying the piano when she was five, interrupted her lessons for her bow to society and then went to Europe to study.

In London she gave a command performance for the late King George the Fifth of England and toured the continent as a concert pianist.

Then Anne's programs were comprised of classical music. But she is proud of her ability to play jazz and believes that every musician today should have some knowledge of it. Her husband Eugene Otto is an artist, too and together they have composed thirty-five songs for their own amusement.

Dear Robert...

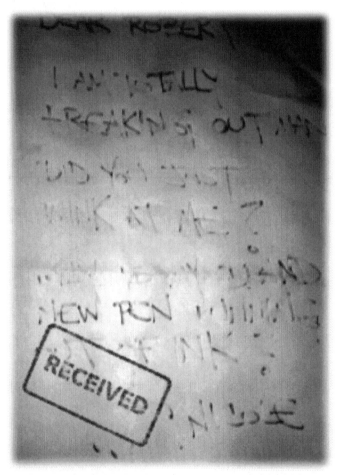

"I am totally freaking out! Did you just wink at me?
Why is my brand new pen running out of ink?"

THE RETURN TO ROBERT

When Minnie Otto fell ill in 1945, Gene and Anne relocated to Key West and moved into the Otto family home. Although Anne and Gene achieved great heights during their decade in New York, family came first. Gene's connections on the small island of Key West, coupled with his reputation among fellow Key West "Conchs" would also prove beneficial to his career as an artist, so the decision was made to move back to his childhood home.

"Besides playing and painting, Gene and I collaborated in writing popular songs. He did the lyrics and I, the music. But it's a competitive business."

Two of the Ottos' songs were published but neither made the hit parade, she said.

An artist with an established reputation, Otto decided to return to his family's two-story, turreted old Conch house when his mother became ill in the 1940s.

His wife carefully packed up their 18th century copper collection and priceless antiques gathered in France and Italy and they headed for home.

In the living-room there's a full-length portrait of Mrs. Otto painted by her husband. It wears a perpetual "No Sale," tag, for it's their favorite painting

Minnie passed away at 9:45 pm on September 14, 1945. Gene held her hand as she drew her last breath. Anne played a requested song on the grand piano downstairs. All of Minnie's children were present for a death that marked the end of an era for the home at 534 Eaton Street. The estate was divided between the Otto children, but Joseph, Thomas, and Mizpah signed their shares over to Gene and Anne, thereby ushering in a new chapter of their lives.

It was Gene's turn to shine as an artist, while Anne put her music on the back burner and rekindled the homemaking skills she had learned at The Garland School. Anne didn't appear to mind trading her piano career to play second fiddle to Gene at first, but it was a decision she would eventually regret.

And then there was the doll.

Anne & Gene pose with one of their Yorkshire Terriers in Key West. Three dogs and a Key deer are interred at the Otto plot, but Anne is notably absent.

Anne met Robert shortly after Minnie Otto's passing. Although Anne was no stranger to Gene's eccentricities, loveable quirks became cause for concern when her forty-five-year-old husband resumed playing with dolls. Gene's behavior was described by Scott Eyman in a *Sun Sentinel* article:

"He built a special attic room for Robert, complete with its own correctly proportioned furniture and toys. He would often go up to the attic to spend time with his doll, and it was about this time, in the 1940s, that stories about Robert began to leak out of the house."

One popular story came from a plumber doing work in the attic who heard giggling coming from behind him. When he turned around, the doll had moved across the room. The plumber fled the house, never to return.

Friends and neighbors close to the family confirm the reports. Myrtle Reuter, who would eventually become the doll's caretaker, revealed:

"A neighbor told me Anne told him that whenever Gene did anything mean or hateful he always blamed it on the doll."

But to paint Gene as a cruel eccentric would be a disservice to the man and his legacy. Key West knew Gene as an accomplished artist, architect, and native son who cared deeply about his community, gave freely of his time and knew how to get things done. Most of the community knew nothing of Robert, but Gene was never one to share the spotlight when it was his turn to shine.

THIS INDENTURE, Made this 16th day of October, A. D. 1945, between MIZPAH OTTO de BOE and MICHAEL PRICE de BOE, her husband, JOSEPH OTTO and NANCY ROSE OTTO, his wife, and THOMAS OSGOOD OTTO, JR., and MARJORIE FALES OTTO, his wife, all of the County of Dade, in the State of Florida, parties of the first part, and ROBERT EUGENE OTTO and ANNETTE PARKER OTTO, husband and wife, whose permanent address is 534 Eaton Street, Key West, Florida, of the County of Monroe, in the State of Florida, parties of the second part (the said Mizpah Otto de Boe being one and the same person as Misphla Otto, and the said Misphla Otto, Joseph Otto, Thomas Osgood Otto, Jr., and Robert Eugene Otto being the four children and heirs at law of Thomas O. Otto, deceased, who died intestate on the 21st day of March, A. D. 1917, a resident of Monroe County, Florida),

WITNESSETH, that the said parties of the first part, for and in consideration of the sum of Ten Dollars and other valuable considerations, to them in hand paid by the said parties of the second part, the receipt whereof is hereby acknowledged, have granted, bargained and sold to the said parties of the second part, their heirs and assigns forever, their undivided three-fourths (3/4) interest in and to the following described land, situate, lying and being in the County of Monroe, State of Florida, to-wit:

In the City of Key West, according to Whitehead's Map of 1829. Is part of Lot Number two (2) in Square Number Thirty-seven (37) lying on the East side of Eaton Street;
Commencing at a point Forty-two (42) feet from the S. W. corner of Simonton and Eaton Streets, and running thence along on Eaton Street in a S. W'ly direction Forty-two (42) feet; thence at right angles in a S. E'ly direction One hundred (100) feet; thence at right angles in a N. E'ly direction Forty-two (42) feet; thence at right angles in a N. W'ly direction One hundred (100) feet to place of beginning on Eaton Street;

And the said parties of the first part do hereby fully warrant the title to said land; and will defend the same against the lawful claims of all persons whomsoever.

County documents show Gene's siblings signing their shares of the family home over to Eugene and Annette on October 16. 1945 after the death of their mother. Minnie Otto. on September 14th.

103

These 2013 photos show the attic room where Robert lived and the adjacent plumbing job that remains unfinished to this day. Robert's room was furnished with wooden chairs, tables and benches scaled to Robert's size. A cedar wardrobe chest held a selection of costumes for the doll. The space is used for storage today, but an effigy of Robert remains in the room as a tribute to the time the doll spent at 534 Eaton St.

Dear Robert...

Dear Robert,

I'm writing to apologize to you for taking so many pictures without asking for your permission when I was there in May. I'm sorry for not believing and for acting so brazen. Please forgive me.

Traveling has been trying since we were there 3 months ago. Of course we had flight delays on our way home. My business travel had troubles as well. Also, my sister's car broke down on the way to our family reunion and someone stole one of her bikes from the bike rack. She was a day late showing up.

K.B. totaled her car about a month ago. A week later she fell and broke 6 ribs. She became addicted to the pain medication she was on for 10 days and had to go through terrible withdrawals.

I've just been told that I'm going to be laid off from the new job I had just started when we visited.

Many other bad things have happened since that day... I don't know if you're behind them. I ask that you accept my heartfelt apology and refrain from any further negative actions and to please remove any harmful spells that may have been cast.

Most Sincerely,

Tales From The Turret

Life gives lemons...

When life gives you lemons, make lemonade. When Robert gives you lemons, return them and apologize.

Jessica Schreckengost-Nauman managed the Artist House and is no stranger to the inn's ghostly charms. Her maiden name means "frightened by ghosts," and though she has seen her fair share of ghostly happenings, not once have the ghosts of the inn frightened her.

Jessica purchased half a dozen bright yellow decorative lemons for the guesthouse in 2010. They sat in a glass bowl near the reception desk. She had no reason for the purchase; she just believed they seemed right.

It didn't take long for the lemons to start disappearing. One at a time they would go, only to be returned by guests as they headed to breakfast or during checkout. No one provided an explanation; they would just place the errant lemons back in the bowl.

Jessica eventually put the lemons away. A month later, the Artist House received a package with no name, no note and no return address—just a lemon. Jessica was perplexed. Several months later, a guest asked if she had seen the letter to Robert at the East Martello Museum. "What letter is that?" she asked.

The full letter appears on the next page. Robert is blamed, but it should be noted that Anne is probably due credit in the case of the disappearing lemons. An interview with her close friend revealed that one of Anne's specialty desserts was a lemon pie she sometimes prepared for potential buyers of Gene's artwork when they came for dinner at the Artist House.

Fort East Martello Museum and Gardens
3501 S. Roosevelt Blvd.
Key West, Florida 33040

January 5, 2011

Dear Museum Curator,

It has taken some time to write this letter but I feel that I must share our experience that we encountered with Robert the Doll.

We visit beautiful Key West every summer in June and we always stay at the Artist House B&B where Eugene grew up with Robert. We have visited Robert at the museum many times and have read all the letters posted on the wall from tourists stating the bad luck encountered when not asking Robert's permission to take his picture. We have asked his permission, have taken pictures and have never had a problem. We dismissed this as just a tale, until our last visit.

While staying in the turret suite at the Artist House we experienced something different. Out of curiosity, we wondered what the attic looked like above us where Robert was discovered before he came to the museum. My husband and I slowly climbed the attic steps and opened the hatch door. We poked our heads thru peering into the dark, taking pictures, hoping to photograph an orb or something. Anything? All we saw was old furniture stored away. The next day we checked out of our room and did some last minute shopping. While walking around town, I began to feel very ill, feverish and my legs began tingling in pain. We got into our car and headed home. We made the 5 hour trip with no problems. The next day I woke with an unusual pain. I lifted my shirt and my side torso had a serious painful rash. I went to the doctor and was diagnosed with shingles. The following day my husband began feeling ill, doubled over in cramps and pain. He was diagnosed with kidney stones.

Now you may be wondering, what does this have to do with Robert? All this seems to fit together in the event that followed. While finally unpacking our bags, I got to the bottom of my suitcase and wrapped up in one of my shirts was a plastic artificial lemon. You see in the hallway at the Artist House was a beautiful bowl with artificial lemons set out as a display. I remembered seeing them and commenting on the display. Somehow one single lemon made its way into my suitcase. I did not put it there. My husband did not put it there. Maybe Robert did? I thought how strange. I placed the lemon on the counter at our home. A few weeks went by and my husband and I were still very ill. Then it dawned on me.... was this Robert's way of getting us back for goofing around in his home and not asking to enter his attic. I immediately placed the lemon in a box and mailed it back to the Artist House with no explanation. I did not want them you think we had taken it. Once that lemon was out of our home I began feeling better, the pain from the shingles subsided and my husband passed his kidney stones.

You may read this letter and think....what a crazy story. It is crazy but it is true. I write this letter in hopes that you will post this on your wall near Robert and it will serve as a reminder that Robert has this thing about him, he is intriguing, devilish, mischievous and still playing tricks to this day.

Signed

True Believers
SW Florida

GENE OTTO: ARTIST

At 45 years old, Gene had no time to waste making a name for himself and creating the legacy he so desired. Gene's schooling in Paris and study of the great masters led to a style that was all his own. His palettes were filled with green hues and bright whites that he combined to capture the faded facades of Key West as they appeared under the ever-present, harsh, tropical sunlight.

Gene held shows in New York and Miami, where he proved his versatility with landscapes, still life paintings, leatherworking, and portraits. He made his biggest impact at home in Key West. Newspaper articles raved about his art openings in the society pages, each one being bigger than the last with a guest list that included the most prominent residents of Key West. Gene was also an active member of the community, lending support to the Key West Woman's Club and Garden Club as well as assisting with the design of numerous landmarks. Art remained Gene's passion, and the Otto home came to serve as a showplace for Gene's artistic creations.

Unsold works of art adorned the walls throughout the home, accented by the expensive furniture the Ottos acquired in Europe and rare curios of copper bowls and ceramic cows that Gene often featured in his still life paintings. Gene's driving force was the idea that his home would one day become a museum dedicated to his life's work as an artist. In describing his vision to Anne, he asked that she cast his hands in wax upon his death and make 'The Artist's Hands" the centerpiece of his museum.

A neighbor who was close with Anne disclosed that Gene put every cent he made back in to elements of the house he felt would serve this vision. Together, they would entertain guests—Anne preparing her famous chicken and rice or Ropa Viaja and lemon pie, Gene showing off his art in hopes of a sale. Although Gene frowned on the consumption of alcohol, wine was served to dinner guests; hard liquor was forbidden. Anne, on the other hand, kept a bottle of 'special water' in the refrigerator that Gene was told not to touch. Apparently, he had no idea Anne was filling the bottle with vodka at a neighbor's house and enjoying a few belts most evenings after Gene went to sleep. Many nights she would sit on top of the cistern at the back of the property and gossip with her next-door neighbor, but each morning she returned to her role as the artist's wife.

Thursday, December 21, 1963   THE KEY WEST CITIZEN   Page 3

Gene Ottos Combine Backgrounds Of France, Key West In Homestead Expressive Of Artistic Achievements

Neighborliness In Key West

HEARTWARMING to all Floridians is the story of Key West's Gene Otto. He was born in the Island City. His life and work are so intertwined with his home town that his paintings are recognizable anywhere. His distinctive palette of muted colors reflects the sunny glare which is the usual light of Key West.

His love for "things Key West" has prompted Mr. Otto to do much more than paint. He has staged eight of his city's flower shows with such skill that they won coverage by magazines, including the National Geographic. His hand is visible in the design or coloring of nearly a dozen landmarks in the southernmost community of the United States mainland.

Most pleasing of all is the report of Herald Staff Writer Jean Wardlow: "The prophet without honor has nothing to do with Artist Gene Otto. His homefolks are crazy about him." They should be. And we hope his example will be followed by many in other parts of Florida. They, too, will earn the affection of their neighbors.

prophet is without honor in his home land" can well be changed in respect to Eugene Otto to "an artist is without recognition in his home land."

There is not a handful of Key Westers, many of whom knew Gene when he daubed in water colors at the Hargrove Institute during his elementary school days, who

OTTO know that today at 45 he has come into his own and, with a definite charm that is distinctively his own, has served notice that in the year to come he will take his rightful place among our successful contemporary American artist.

Gene worked as an antiquary in New York to obtain funds with which to pursue his art studies. After attending the Academy of Fine Arts in Chicago and Art Students league in New York, he traveled to Paris, advancing his knowledge of oils at the Academy Colarossi, La Grande Chaumiere and Acadamie Julien.

During all the years of his schooling, Gene worked toward a goal: Purity of tone. To accomplish this difficult task which he set for himself, shadows had to be eliminated from his canvas.

REACHING GOAL

Now at 45 he is confident that he is attaining the goal he set for himself.

Earlier this year he returned to Key West with his wife, Anne, because of the serious illness of his mother. With time on his hands he put onto canvas six Key West landscapes.

One of the best is a landscape painted from a tower room of the Otto home in Eaton st., just a few feet away from the bedroom where the artist was born.

PLANS NEW YORK SHOW

He is getting together enough work on the Key West scene for a New York showing. He had a small exhibition in Miami last winter.

He recently completed negotiations for purchase of the Otto homestead and will make his future home here and in New York.

He is a brother of former Dade and Monroe counties Circuit Court Judge Joseph Otto, now practicing law in Miami; Col. Thomas Osgood Otto, USA, Miami surgeon, and Mrs. Michael Price de Boe of Coral Gables.

112

Portrait of
A COMPLETE ARTIST

All is not paint and canvas with Gene Otto. For Key West, he has:

DESIGNED the entrance of Martello Gallery and Museum and spent eight months with a carpenter, designing and building the bird cage and pavilion of the West Martello Museum.

STAGED eight of Key West's flower shows, which have been featured in magazines, including National Geographic.

EXECUTED all the colors for the city electric plant and the new city hall.

DESIGNED the interior of the Convention Hall in Old Mallory Square and supervised its restoration, and did the same for the interior of the Hospitality House.

DESIGNED an outdoor reading room for the Monroe County Public Library.

ARRANGED and designed the brick garden of the Key West Women's Club and helped with the building's restoration, and designed the Museum of the Fish of the Key West Waters Museum.

Record Crowd Of Art Viewers Attends Gene Otto Reception

Artist's Civic Work Extolled

Paintings by Otto Draw Hundreds-- And Compliments

30-E THE MIAMI HERALD Sunday, February 14, 1954

Conchs Love Gene Otto's Paintings of Key West

Dear Robert...

On August 5, 2011 me and my wife went to go see you. I was warned not to take your picture. I thought it was all mumbo-jumbo, so I took your picture without asking permission.

The next day I went snorkeling and got stung 3 times by Portuguese manowar. There were about 50 of them in the water and I was the only one who got stung. The next day was my birthday. I had a few drinks. I came to several hours later in the emergency room getting my arm stitched, handcuffed to a hospital bed. I had completely blacked out.

Apparently in my blackout I had wandered away from my hotel over to another hotel and broke a window with my elbow. When the cops showed up I ran. It took them quite a while to catch me. When I was finally apprehended I was apparently speaking in a Caribbean accent. I don't remember any of this. This is all based on the police report and what I was told by the deputies.

I now have to come back for a court date. I was charged with criminal mischief. I was arrested on my birthday on my honeymoon. On our way back home our flights were delayed several times. It just felt like you played a huge prank on me for taking your picture without permission.

THE ARTIST'S WIFE

A 1962 *Miami Herald* article starts, *"Thirty-seven years ago, Annette Parker Otto traded a grand piano and a budding career as a concert pianist-composer for the role of an artist's wife. 'And Gene's career has come first with me ever since,' she said smiling."*

It is difficult to imagine the smile being sincere, but newspaper reports from the 1950s and 1960s depict an Otto family content within their roles; he as a famous artist, and she as a devoted wife. Jo Ellen Keller shed light on the Otto's arrangement in a 1953 Society feature in the *Key West Citizen*. Although rumors of Gene's physical abuse of Anne are false, a pattern of mental cruelty by today's standards was beginning to emerge. Here are some excerpts from the column:

- *"Paris was the prelude that drew Bostonian Anne Parker and Key Wester Gene Otto into the harmony of an art and a marriage shared and understood."*

- *"Though, like all artists, Gene Otto is an entity unto himself, his dominance in the field of painting is at least partly attributed to his dominant role in his own household."*

- *"Anne Otto gave up her career in music though she had found considerable success."*

- *"She found her true fulfillment in her husband's career in Key West and has done a rather stunning job of finding her métier in being a gifted homemaker and superb cook."*

- *"While Anne Otto graciously fills many requests made by Key West clubs and organizations, her husband has produced a genre of painting that is entirely his own and has brought him acclaim as a Key West artist."*

Stories from those closest to Anne shed even more light on her relationship with Gene.

- *"Anne had a presence that radiated wherever she went. Gene couldn't stand being overshadowed, so he made Anne wait outside for five minutes when they arrived at public events so he could be the center of attention."*

- *"Anne wanted to play piano at church, but Gene was so jealous of her talents he refused to let her play anywhere but in their home. The military boys used to line up outside the Otto home just to hear her play."*

- *"Gene was very dry. He was an eccentric and everything had to be his way in the house. They had shelves with copper pots, and if she dusted, he would notice one even slightly out of place. He had photos made to show her where things went."*

Anne and Gene had separate bedrooms, and although her close friends insist that Gene adored her, it is hard to look at the bigger picture and not believe his motives were self-serving from the start. Unfortunately, this would not become clear to Anne until after Gene's death.

Famous Key Lime Pie

Mrs. Gene Otto keeps house in the home on Eaton St. in which her husband was born. Her kitchen has two ranges ("I never have enough burners on one," she said), copper molds and cabinet doors decorated by her husband. He is a well-known artist.

Her cookery style is Conch and Cuban with French touches learned when they lived in Paris.

Mrs. Otto also is a master at streamlining old recipes. Her doctored b o t t l e d mayonnaise tastes like homemade French or Spanish mayonnaise. She uses canned roast beef in Ropa Vieja.

She learned to make lime pie from her late mother-in-law.

"Gene's mother always s a i d four eggs for family, six for company," said Ann Otto.

Key Lime Pie

4 egg yolks, beaten slightly
1 can sweetened condensed milk
juice of 7 large key limes (about ½ cup)
9-inch baked pie shell
4 egg whites
4 tablespoons sugar

Combine egg yolks and condensed milk and mix well. Add juice and blend well. Turn into shell. Bake in a medium oven (350 degrees) until set, 10 to 15 minutes. Meanwhile, beat egg whites until stiff. Gradually beat in sugar and beat very stiff. Put on pie by spoonfuls, spreading to edge of shell all around. Place in oven (400 degrees) for 5 minutes. Reduce heat to 300 degrees. Bake until meringue is pale colored.

Mrs. Otto has added her own improvisations to Ropa Vieja.

She adds celery, "but nobody else would," she admits.

She also serves it ceremoniously, first a spoonful of grits on the plate, then a hunk of butter and diced medium-aged Cheddar cheese, then the hot meat.

A true marriage of Conch and Cuban cookery.

Ropa Vieja

1 12-ounce can roast beef
2 tablespoons olive oil
1 large onion, diced
3 cloves garlic, finely chopped
2 or 3 stalks celery with leaves, chopped very fine
1 10-ounce can tomatoes
1 large green pepper, cut coarsely
2 tablespoons worcestershire sauce
3 dashes seasoned salt
Lots of freshly ground pepper
1 2-ounce bottle olives, sliced

Shred beef finely, tearing into stringy pieces with fingers. Remove any fat from meat. Place oil in frying pan and heat. Add onion, garlic and celery and cook slowly until soft. Add juice and about half the tomato from the can. (Save remaining tomato for other uses.) Simmer about 15 minutes. Add meat and mix well. Add green pepper, worcestershire, seasoned salt and black pepper. Cover and simmer over low heat about 3 hours, to allow flavors to completely penetrate meat. Nearly all liquid should be absorbed. About 10 minutes before serving add olives. Serve with grits with butter and cheese. Makes 2 to 3 servings.

* * *

Mrs. Otto's doctored mayonnaise makes a salad of shrimp or most anything else taste extra special.

Doctored Mayonnaise

1 pint good quality commercial mayonnaise
2 tablespoons olive oil
1 tablespoon wine vinegar
1 to 2 cloves garlic, crushed
2 bird peppers (tiny hot peppers)
3 dashes seasoned salt

Add olive oil and vinegar to mayonnaise and blend. Add garlic and peppers, pressed through a small strainer. Add seasoned salt and blend. Makes about 1 pint.

* * *

Below is another of Mrs. Cobo's recipes. This is for picadillo and is to be served with rice. It is a little more moist than the stuffing for canapes given in columns 1 and 2 on this page.

Picadillo

1 green pepper, chopped
1 large onion, chopped
3 to 4 cloves garlic, finely chopped
1 tablespoon lard
1 1-pound can tomatoes
1 bay leaf
¼ cup raisins
2 tablespoons capers
2 tablespoons chopped olives
1 to 1½ teaspoons olive brine
1½ pounds ground beef
Salt

Cook green pepper, onion and garlic in fat until soft. Add tomatoes and bay leaf. Simmer about 15 minutes. Add raisins, capers, olives and olive brine. Simmer a few minutes. Add beef and simmer 20 to 30 minutes. Serve over white rice. Makes 4 servings.

Annette Otto's culinary talents are highlighted in a *Miami Herald* food feature that includes her recipes for Key Lime Pie and Ropa Vieja.

Dear Robert...

I was a recent visitor to the museum on a ghost tour. Our guide led us to the room where Robert the Doll is located. He told us about the "rules" to follow if we wanted to take a photo of Robert. I told Robert my name, asked permission to take the photo and thanked Robert. I thought I had followed the rules.

Later that night, my bottom lip had swollen to twice its size. I also developed a rash on both arms and hands. This lasted a couple of days before I decided to check and see if "Robert did it". I got my iPad and looked up Robert the Doll on the Internet. I did not find anything that suggested I had not followed the rules.

As I closed the tab, I noticed another tab with no title on it. I opened this tab and this is what it said and the only thing on the page.

"You did not say where you were from."

I don't know if I missed hearing this rule or if Robert just wanted to know.

120

Tales From The Turret

Breakfast isn't served...

Sometimes a ghost doesn't appear as a ghost, but blends in as a one of the living, or in the case of the Artist House, as an employee.

Jessica Schreckengost had friends getting married in Key West. Naturally, they stayed at the Artist House. Prior to the wedding, the soon-to-be newlyweds emerged from their room hoping to grab a bite to eat before breakfast started. They were greeted in the kitchen by someone they assumed was a staff member and explained they were looking to get an early start. The woman coldly replied that breakfast was over.

The couple was perplexed, but headed into town. Breakfast was being served at the inn when they returned and they mentioned their experience to Jessica. Wedding guests occupied all of the rooms at the inn, breakfast had not even started at the time of their encounter, and the employee preparing breakfast was shopping at the local grocery store when they were told they were late.

The account could easily be written off as a visitor to the house, someone dropping off flyers, or maybe a vendor of some sort, but this is just the latest case of someone encountering a seemingly human presence that took a certain degree of ownership in the house.

Linda Haas worked at the Artist House for several years in the late '90s and had several encounters with a woman she believes to be Anne.

"Sometimes I would see her drinking tea in the back garden and other times she looked into the rooms as if she was supervising me and making sure everything was okay. She always had that smile I couldn't figure out. I'd think she was a guest for a second, but inside I knew. She was always heading off through the kitchen to the backyard."

THE DEATH
OF AN ARTIST

June 24, 1974 was a sad day in Key West. An obituary in the *Key West Citizen* that week announced the death of Eugene Otto.

Prominently placed, the death notice praised the many accomplishments in Gene's life, recalled his dedication to community and impact on the city, and painted a fine tribute that would have made the artist proud.

Death did not come quickly for Gene. His obituary referenced a long illness, which family documents would later confirm was caused by Parkinson's disease—a degenerative disorder of the central nervous system.

Although there is no mention of Robert the Doll in Gene's obituary, a *Sun Sentinel* article published a decade after his death sheds light on Gene's final days with the doll:

"In the months preceding his death, as his health failed, he spent most of his time in the attic room, talking to Robert."

Anne would shortly confirm that Gene and the doll were very close, but we may never know if the final months they spent talking in the attic were a result of the delusional psychosis suffered by more than a quarter of patients with Parkinson's disease, or the actions of a man seeking comfort from his oldest and dearest friend.

Gene took his final breath in a Miami hospital and was buried beside his beloved Yorkshire Terriers in the Otto family's Key West plot.

Deaths .7/57

Eugene Otto dies

By EARL R. ADAMS
Citizen staff writer

Eugene Otto, native Key West artist who contributed much to the cultural life of Key West, died in Miami Monday after a long illness.

The youngest of three sons born to Mr. and Mrs. Thomas Otto, both native Key Westers, he devoted many hours to making Key West a more attractive place in which to live.

Quiet and at times unassuming, he became carried away when engaged in a project that he felt would benefit and prove attractive to mankind. Then words would pour forth which was completely opposite to the slow methodical way he painted.

From designing brick gardens and staging flower shows to personally hanging mounted fish in the museum in Mallory Square, he worked for the city, than which he said there was none better.

Otto grew up in Key West and then struck out on his own to make a name for himself in the art galleries of the United States and Europe.

land, a key in which the colors wince in the heat and blanch in the luminosity until his very canvas takes on a feeling of his subject."

He was never too busy with his art work to assist in Key West development and beautification programs.

Nominated by the Key West Woman's Club for his advice and assistance to that organization, he was awarded The Citizen's Community Service Award for 1964.

In their nomination of the talented native Key West, the clubwomen said: "There is no history of community improvement over a period of many years that has not benefited by the ready assistance and the sharing of the fine talent of this man."

Among his civic achievements were his assistance in the reconstruction of East Martello Gallery, designing and supervising the building of the pavilion and bird cage at the gallery and acting as a consultant for the decorating and furnishing of the new City Hall.

He spent many hours of

Eugene Otto's obituary describes a community driven artist with numerous achievements but does not have a single mention of the doll.

125

and Europe

He studied at the Academy of Fine Arts in Chicago and the Art Students League in New York before traveling to Europe where he developed a definite palette, which he repeated over and over was exclusively his own.

He was abroad for eight years and his last four years were spent at the Academy Julienne.

It was while painting and continuing his studies in Paris that he met Annette Parker, a native of Boston, who was studying music in at that time. They were married in Paris on May 3, 1930.

With Mrs. Otto's music studies over and ready to launch out on his career as a painter of still life and landscapes, Otto returned to the picturesque frame dwelling at 534 Eaton Street where he was born on October 25, 1900.

His unusual colors and precision of landscapes in which objects were isolated, painted in the glare of the blazing Key West sunlight, won for him acclaim in the art world.

Author Philip Wylie, an admirer of his work, once remarked: "I kept having the feeling I should put on my sunglasses."

He best summed up the work of this native Key Wester when he said: "He has found a new key in which to relect the light-soaked new City Hall.

He gave many hours of voluntary work to the Woman's Club. The bricked-in garden and patio of their clubhouse was his design and he also had a hand in the restoring and decorating of the club house. He designed and supervised the making of the sign that hangs in the entrance to that building.

Nine of the successful flower shows, which became nationally known and brought recognition from National Geographic and Life Magazine, were staged by him.

He contributed many hours to the restoring of Mallory Squre.

The beautiful and educational fish museum in the Chamber of Commerce was designed by him.

Gene Otto laid aside his brushes several years ago because of illness. He will paint no more, but his contributions to the city where his grandfather, Dr. Joseph Otto, a refugee from Prussia at the time of the student's revolution, came here in 1877 as contract surgeon for the United States Army, will be a lasting monument to his devotion.

Beside his widow, Annette, he leaves a sister Mizpah Price (Mrs. Michael) de Boe; and one brother, Joseph Otto, a former Circuit Court Judge.

Funeral arrangments which are in charge of Lopez Funeral Home will be announced later.

The family requests that memorial gifts be made to the Monroe County Public Library to be used in the creation of an art department.

Eugene Otto obituary. continued from previous page. Otto's obituary originally appeared in the *Key West Citizen* on June 25, 1974.

Dear Robert...

Dear Robert The Doll,

I just wanted to thank you for all of the good luck you brought me. I took your picture without asking permission because I didn't believe you were anything other than a raggedy old child's plaything, although now I'm a believer. Things have changed for the better now that I have your picture, and to me you're no longer just an ugly rag, but a cuddly old doll all stuffed up with love. If you weren't a doll I think we could be friends.

A demon, really...and your role is supposedly to teach people to ask permission. So that like makes you the demon in charge of good manors? Just a thought, but I suspect you sat in the wrong classroom, didn't do very well in demon school, or simply pissed someone off that they gave you that job.

Regardless, I think you're pretty cool.

Thanks again you big bad demon you.

███████████

127

A WOMAN SCORNED

What happened to Anne after Gene's death is nothing short of tragic. When Gene died, Anne discovered she had been written out of her husband's will. Everything was left to his sister, Mizpah.

Although Anne would never know the reasons why this had happened, Gene's sister would later claim Gene was hurt because he had been written out of Annette's mother's will and received nothing from her estate.

Anne's best friend and neighbor, William Gaiser, drove her to Miami where they begged Mizpah to at least let Anne keep the house. A later letter from Gene's sister claims the house was left to Anne all along, but Mizpah was creative in her written accounts. She laid claim to all of the valuable antiques the Ottos had collected during their time in Paris—antiques that would have freed Anne from money troubles for the rest of her life.

Eventually, Anne sold the house to William Gaiser and moved back to Massachusetts to live with her sister Lester. When asked about arrangements for her husband's gravesite, she made a point of not giving the deceased artist any satisfaction. She had Gene's plot covered in concrete rather than brick. "It's good enough for him," she is quoted as saying.

Anne also gave Robert the Doll to William Gaiser before she left, saying, "That doll was Gene's best friend. Of course, he never had any other friends."

To this day, Gaiser wishes he had burned the doll. He insists there is nothing to Robert. It is just a doll that has overshadowed the beauty, talent, charm, and class of his friend Annette. But William did not burn the doll. He left it in the second floor cedar chest for his friend Myrtle Reuter, for whom he had bought the house.

Anne left Key West facing the reality that she had thrown away her own career and dreams in favor of a man who her family had always claimed was only after her money. As a final insult, even her request for a portrait Gene had painted of her was refused; Anne had wanted to pass the painting on to her niece.

Anne would spend her last five years in Massachusetts before dying of pancreatic cancer and a broken heart. Her departure from the house ushered in a new era for Robert the Doll.

Annette Parker Otto lived out her final years with her sister in this home on Barretts Mill Road in Concord. Massachusetts.

A letter from Gene's sister Mizpah to her niece and nephew provides her version of why Annette was written out of Gene's will. The document was discovered in the Otto family archives and provides important details that were previously unknown.

August 11, 1974

Thomas O. Otto, III,
Executor of Will of Mizpah Otto deBoe,
1635 W. 27th St.,
Sunset Isle #2,
Miami Beach, Fla. 33140

Dearest Tommy and Carol:

I want you to know the truth about your Uncle Eugene's Will. He was disinherited by Mrs. Parker's Will. He said that she had left her will to her two daughters, Lester and Annette, and the remainder of her estate to her two grandchildren, Annette and Tom Mott Shaw.

Annette felt very hurt at the time when the desk Mrs. Parker had always promised to her as a child, she gave to her granddaughter Annette. Eugene was disinherited by Mrs. Parker's Will although he was married to Annette, and moreover Annette felt very hurt over this. When Lester moved her mother into a nursing home, she moved all Mrs. Parker's furnishings to her home in Concord. Your Uncle Eugene did not mind this as he always felt himself to be an outsider in the Parker family. He was not welcomed like your father was into the Fales family, as a member of it. Besides, he was not interested in New England American furniture. He was making his own collection of European things. When Annette returned from her mother's funeral she did not bring a piece of silver or linen back with her.

Eugene was never interested in a piece of her family jewelry. After your Aunt Annette's operation two days before Christmas, 1972, she was nervous and depressed following that operation. I knew,and its prognosis that she needed a diversion and long rest with Lester. Meanwhile Eugene was ill with Parkinson's disease, was very worried and longing for her. And after coming from Green Briar and moving me home, she left the next morning and she made it a very happy occasion for me. She was to visit with Lester for two weeks but she stayed six weeks. Eugene felt very ill and worried. Miss Nesbitt said, "How he loved Mrs. Otto." Miss Nesbitt said when she saw how Eugene was grieving for Mrs. Otto she told him that Mrs. Otto was coming back from her visit in the north and he answered dejectedly, "I hope so."

We took care of him here and comforted him all we could. It was during that period that he made his Will, 1973, leaving the house to Annette, which was jointly owned, but its contents were left to me. This included his life collection of 18th century China painted Cows, and its beautiful copper pieces that he had found in an old Chateau in France, which he cherished, his Louis XIVE desk I had selected for him, from Mary Allbert Hinton and his Antiques (when they were in business together), called Arts Decoratifs.

131

There were a number of five chairs and other pieces that he inherited from Mary Albert Hinton when he acted as executor of her estate. As Mr. Wilson Trammell knows we had planned in my Will, to leave our family portraits and my pieces of furniture which he had purchased for me in Paris, Doctor deBoe's desk, this three little director rustic chairs and other pieces which he selected for Doctor deB e and me in Paris.

I kept his confidence secret from Annette about his Will that I could not betray his trust. When she learned of it, it was no doubt a terrible shock to her, but as you know you had negotiated these treasures that Eugene had willed to me, in exchange for my possession of Eugene's portrait of Annette. I signed the release paper in your presence, Tommy.

This is the only portrait your Uncle Gene ever painted. I know he was a landscape and still life painter, but he did this portrait in the full glory of the vigor and love of her. He will rub her arm and comment on the beauty of the color of her skin. Vittorio said he got the rose glow of her skin that Giorgioni had. To me it is a Masterpiece, and it is a Gene Otto glow. Annette was hurt because she could not give it to her niece, Annette Shaw and her namesake, as a gift.

Your Uncle Eugene knew the value of the treasures he was leaving and that the sale of his and your Aunt Annette's home would bring enough to keep her comfortably provided for.

Aunt Mizpah

The letter above details Anne's thwarted wish to give the portrait Gene painted of her to a niece. Gene only painted one portrait in his life (pictured left). He was quick to correct that 'Anne in Her New Hat' is a painting, not a portrait. The location of both artworks is unknown. If you have information on their location, contact david@phantompress.com

Robert Did It!
The Third Tenant...

Two men who rented at the Otto House in the mid-1970s had regular encounters with the doll Their story was shared with The Sun Sentinal in 1985.

"There was constant noise coming from the room. Sometimes it was like little kids laughing and other times like someone rummaging around. When it first started happening we would go upstairs to check it out, but always found nothing. It was only after a half dozen times that we realized the doll had moved. At first we blamed each other and laughed it off as a practical joke. Sometimes the doll's head would be looking in a different direction, other times its arms were propped up around the chair, and once its legs were even crossed. It started happening with greater frequency and we realized this was no joke."

They invited Malcolm Ross to see the doll in his room. Ross felt as if he was entering some kind of strange force field.

"It was like a metal bar running down my back. At first when we walked through the door, the look on his face was like a little boy being punished. It was as if he was asking himself, 'Who are these people in my room and what are they going to do to me?'"

Ross's friends told him Robert's backstory and pointed out the children's furniture. It was at this point that Malcolm noticed a change in the doll's expression, as if he was following the conversation. When one of the men made a comment about what an old fool Gene Otto must have been. Robert's expression turned to one of disdain.

"There was some kind of intelligence there. The doll was listening to us."

Annette Otto poses next to one of her husband's most acclaimed paintings, titled: 'Anne in Her New Hat.'

Annette Otto

Annette Otto, widow of the late artist Robert Eugene Otto, died January 9 in Concord, Massachusetts after an extended illness.

She was born December 9, 1902 and spent most of her early years in New England. After graduating from Back Bay School, she specialized in piano at the National Cathedral in Washington, D.C. and later attended the Garland School in Boston. From Boston she went to Paris and London to continue her studies.

While in Paris, she met and married Robert Eugene "Gene" Otto, a student of painting on May 3, 1930.

In 1944 the Otto's moved to Key West and resided in the family home at 534 Eaton St.

In 1950 she became associated with the Monroe County Public Library and remained with that institution for many years until her husband's ill health forced her to retire.

Mrs. Otto was a member of Saint Paul's Episcopal Church for many years.

Memorial services will be held Friday at 2 p.m. in Concord, Mass. In lieu of flowers it is requested contributions be made to the cancer society. She is survived by one sister Mrs. L.P. Shaw, who resides at 71 Barretts Mill Rd., Concord, Mass. 01742.

R-309

The Commonwealth of Massachusetts

SECRETARY OF THE COMMONWEALTH

No. ....

OFFICIAL BURIAL (OR REMOVAL) PERMIT

Division of Vital Statistics

(Issued under the provisions of Chapter 114, Section 45, General Laws, Ter. Ed. as amended.)

[This permit can be signed only by the agent of the Board of Health (or in towns where there is no Board of Health by the town clerk) of the city or town in which the death occurred AFTER the FILING and acceptance of a satisfactory certificate of death, printed or typed in durable black ink.]

Concord, ... Jan. 10, 1979
(City or town)   (Date)

A satisfactory certificate of death having been filed, permission is hereby given to
CHARLES W. DEE, Pres.&Treas., Joseph Dee & Son, Inc., Concord, Mass.
(Name)   (Address)

for the removal from .... , and the interment
(To be filled out in case of removal)

at Mt. Auburn .... Cemetery in Cambridge, Mass., of the

body of Annette (Parker) Otto .... who died Jan. 9, 1979
(Give full name of deceased)   (Month) (Day) (Year)

age 76 years, 1 months, 0 days.

Cause of death Acute Pancreatitis

If a U. S. War Veteran, specify what war, organization, etc. No

Residence at time of death 71 Barrett's Mill Rd., Concord, Mass. 01742

....
(Signature of Agent of Board of Health, or, in towns where there is no Board of Health, of Town Clerk)

Annette Parker Otto's final resting place remained a mystery for more than 30 years. Research for this book located her in the Yantic Cemetery in Norwich, Connecticut. Larry Stanford visited the cemetery to confirm cemetery records and discovered Annette's grave hidden beneath a thick layer of grass. Stanford may have been the first visitor to Annette's grave since her death on January 9, 1979.

Tales From The Turret

The blue orb...

Spirits in the Artist House are by no means contained in the building's interior. Nightly ghost tours share the house's haunted history, and guests report sightings ranging from the plausible to the bizarre.

From 1996–2000, the turret room windows were covered with roll-up shades. The shade in the window where Robert once sat would pull back frequently as if someone was watching... someone curious about the people gathered outside. Employees reported regular difficulties keeping one particular turret room shutter opened. A former manager went so far as to screw it to the side of the house, but the following morning it was closed again.

Perhaps the most peculiar event happened on October 25, 2003. Nearly 80 people were gathered in front of the house when a brilliant blue orb descended from the sky. It went through the roof of the guest house, appeared to the crowd as it traveled the front of the house through the balcony and disappeared into the ground. No one realized at the time that October 25th marks Gene Otto's birthday.

Since that event, the blue orb has reappeared on several occasions, most recently in October 2012. Ted Messimer had a group gathered beside the Artist House and was sharing some of the new discoveries about the Otto family. The familiar blue orb dropped from the sky and was captured on camera. Video taken shortly thereafter showed a playful orb circling his head for several minutes. It seemed to be a clear sign that one of the spirits at the Artist House was pleased with the new information uncovered.

PHOTO: KELLY MORRICAL KOHLER

ROBERT REUTER

In the months following Gene Otto's death, 534 Eaton Street was sold to Annette Otto's friend and neighbor, William Gaiser. Gaiser sold the home to his friends, William and Myrtle Reuter. Myrtle would care for Robert for the next 20 years.

THIS instrument prepared by:
Michael H. Cates
Attorney at Law
505 Whitehead Street
Key West, Florida 33040

FORM 1191 Quit Claim Deed — QUIT CLAIM DEED.

executive line   53443 OFF. REC. 589 PAGE 10

This Indenture

Wherever used herein, the term "party" shall include the heirs, personal representatives, successors and / or assigns of the respective parties hereto, the use of the singular number shall include the plural, and the plural the singular, the use of any gender shall include all genders, and, if used, the term "note" shall include all the notes herein described if more than one.

Made this   12th   day of   August   A. D. 1974

Between

WILLIAM H. GAISER, a single man over 18 years of age,

Monroe   and State of   Florida   , of the County of   party of the first part,

and WILLIAM H. REUTER, JR.

Monroe   and State of   Florida   , party of the second part,

Witnesseth, that the said party of the first part, for and in consideration of the sum of -----------TEN AND NO/100------------------- Dollars, in hand paid by the said party of the second part, the receipt whereof is hereby acknowledged, has remised, released and quitclaimed, and by these presents does remise, release and quitclaim unto the said party of the second part all the right, title, interest, claim and demand which the said party of the first part has in and to the following described lot , piece or parcel of land, situate lying and being in the County of Monroe   State of Florida, to wit:

In the City of Key West, according to Whitehead's Map of 1829, Is part of Lot Number two (2) in Square Number Thirty-seven (37) lying on the East side of Eaton Street:

Commencing at a point Forty-two (42) feet from the S. W. corner of Simonton and Eaton Streets, and running thence along on Eaton Street in a S. W'ly direction Forty-two (42) feet; thence at right angles in a S. E'ly direction One Hundred (100) feet; thence at right angles in a N. E'ly direction Forty-two (42) feet; thence at right angles in a N. W'ly direction One Hundred (100) feet to place of beginning on Eaton Street.

To Have and to Hold the same, together with all and singular the appurtenances thereunto belonging or in anywise appertaining, and all the estate, right, title, interest and claim whatsoever of the said party of the first part, either in law or equity, to the only proper use, benefit and behoof of the said party of the second part.

In Witness Whereof, the said party of the first part has hereunto set his hand and seal the day and year first above written.

Signed, Sealed and Delivered In Our Presence:

William H. Gaiser

STATE OF FLORIDA
DOCUMENTARY STAMP TAX
GIFT IN MOTION   = 0 0.30

State of Florida,
County of   MONROE
I HEREBY CERTIFY, That on this day personally appeared before me, an officer duly authorized to administer oaths and take acknowledgments,

WILLIAM H. GAISER, a single man over 18 years of age,

to me well known to be the person described in and who executed the foregoing instrument and he   acknowledged before me that he executed the same freely and voluntarily for the purposes therein expressed.
WITNESS my hand and official seal at   Key West   , County of   Monroe   , and State of Florida, this   12th
day of   August   A. D. 1974

RECORDED IN OFFICIAL RECORDS BOOK
MONROE COUNTY, FLORIDA
RALPH W. WHITE
CLERK OF CIRCUIT COURT
MIDSTATE LEGAL SUPPLY COMPANY

Notary Public, State of Florida
My Commission Expires   8/8/75

Robert Did It!
The Yellow Fever...

Science describes yellow fever as a viral disease transmitted by primates and certain species of mosquito, but at least one past tenant of the Otto House claims he contracted yellow fever from the doll.

Legends tell of a young man who rented a room at the Otto House in the mid-1970s, only to be tormented by the doll. Some accounts have Robert locking him in a room, cornering him and sitting on his chest to hold him down, while others say the doll took over his brain, bringing him to the brink of insanity. Both legends claim the doll gave him yellow fever.

Myrtle Reuter shared a story from the time when she owned the home:

"We went up north for the summer one year and we left a man who was studying to be a lawyer to live in the house while we were gone. He wrote this fantastic story that the doll was Voodoo and locked him up in the attic and he caught yellow fever. I don't remember his name. To me he was some kind of nut."

This is the first-known written claim of Robert causing illness, but it is certainly not the last. Stories about Robert continued to circulate the island through the 1980s with an additional detail added to the tale. The doll was gone.

A *Miami Herald* article indicated persistent rumors of his whereabouts, the most prevalent being that Robert had taken up residence on neighboring Stock Island. Other stories suggested that the doll had left on his own. A *Sun Sentinel* article that ran in 1985 stated:

"The man who had bought the house from Otto's widow died soon thereafter of carbon-monoxide poisoning from a faulty exhaust system in his car... Robert vanished soon after and nobody who now lives in the house has ever heard of him."

The truth of the matter is that Robert had a new companion. Myrtle Reuter knew the Ottos. She worked for Anne Otto's close friend, Bill Gaiser, who bought the house from Anne after Gene died. Bill is still living as this book goes to press, despite the carbon-monoxide claims.

Myrtle and her husband William bought the Otto House from Gaiser in 1974 and Myrtle started caring for the doll. In an interview with Arthur Myers, Myrtle described how on Christmas Eve she used to dress Robert in pajamas and place him by the Christmas tree. The Reuters sold the house in February of 1980 and Myrtle took Robert the Doll with her. They lived at 1722-A Von Phister Street in Key West until Myrtle started having her own strange encounters with Robert. In 1994, Myrtle donated the doll to the Fort East Martello Museum.

Robert the Doll's lesser known residence: After leaving the Artist House, Robert resided with Myrtle Reuter at 1722-A Von Phister Street in Key West. Myrtle would sit Robert on the porch. It was his home from 1980 until 1994 when he was donated to the East Martello Museum.

ROBERT RULES
FORT EAST MARTELLO

1994. 18.0001

RECORD OF DONATION
TO THE

EAST MARTELLO GALLERY & MUSEUM / S. ROOSEVELT BLVD. / KEY WEST, FL 33040 / 305-296-3913

Nature of Gift __Donation__ "Robert"

Title __Doll__ of Gene Otto as Child Early 1900's

Artist __Unknown__ _____ Dates _____

Description/Medium __Straw and Felt ; Doll clothes were
actually Gene Otto ; Lion Doll is Gene Otto__

Classification: _____ Military; __✓__ Social/Political; _____ Economic/Industrial; _____ Natural; _____ Fine Arts

Date of Object __Early 1900's__ ___ Period/School/Tribe/Military Branch _____

Sizes in Inches Without Mat. Frame, Pedestal: Height __41__ Width __17__ Depth __8__

Signature: How _____ Where _____

Condition of Object and Explanation _____
__Termite Damage__

POLICY REGARDING APPRAISALS
It is the policy of the Society not to perform or provide appraisals of any object that may or may not accede to its collec-.
tions. The donor of an object must provide an appraisal valuation prepared in a professional manner. It is understood that if
a valuation is placed on this document without an appraiser's name, or without an attached appraisal document that
becomes part of this official record, that the valuation figure represents only an insurance value for the Society's purposes.

Valuation: $ _____ Appraisal by _____

I have reached agreement with officials of the Key West Art and Historical Society, a non-profit corporation, to donate to
the Society the object described above. As of this date, said object becomes the sole property of the Society.

Donor Signature __Myrtle D. Reuter__ Date __8/19/94__

Name __Myrtle D. Reuter__

Address __1722 A Von Phister__
__Key West__ __296-__

I hereby acknowledge receipt of the object described above as a donation to the Key West Art and Historical Society.

For the Society _____ Date __8/19/94__

Name _____

Title __Director__

Society Copy / Donor Copy   8/78
__may be an article in Solares Hill
some time ago.__

146

It was the morning of August 18, 1994, when former Key West Art & Historical Society Assistant Director, Joe Pais, was called from his office at the back of the Fort East Martello Museum. There was a lady at the front desk wishing to donate an artifact.

Joe approached a woman looking to be in her mid-50s, casually dressed as if she had been doing housework. In her arms was a doll, unwrapped and unprotected. Joe recalls that the doll was in good shape. The two headed back to Joe's office and Myrtle placed the doll in his chair on Joe's desk.

"This is Robert. He is part of the Otto family. I can't stand him being in my house anymore."

Reuter went on to describe how she locked Robert in a room after noticing that he moved on his own. After the incident, she claimed Robert locked her in a room.

"He's haunted," she told Joe.

Joe saw the value in the treasure and suggested she might want to keep it, but Myrtle went into a frenzy.

"She didn't want to sell it. She didn't want anything in exchange. She wanted it out of her possession."

"That doll has to leave the house," she insisted. Reuter filled out the necessary paperwork and took off quickly. She died less than three months later.

Joe Pais began to make his own discoveries about Robert.

"I placed him in a small, antique chair in my office, directly opposite my desk. He seemed comfortable in the chair. I often looked up in his direction and he always stared back in an un-childlike way. Robert always seemed on the verge of stepping from his chair and I always got the impression that he had moved his chair a few inches to the left and then back to the right. I chalked a mark at the foot of one of the chair legs to find if he was moving the chair but cleverly, he avoided being caught."

Joe shared an office with Museum Director, Susan Olsen.

"Susan did not like the doll. She worked at night and refused to be in the office if Robert was there. It was hard to tell if the doll was moving or not. We would find it slumped down it its chair. Susan was freaked, so we moved the doll to our artifact storage room."

For the next two years, Robert was only available by appointment, but by mid-1996, a local ghost tour was encouraging guests to pay a visit to the doll. Museum staff was afraid of Robert. Employees would often suggest people come back on a day they were not working, or place the responsibility of retrieving Robert on a co-worker. As the number of people requesting time with Robert increased, he was placed on permanent display. Ever since, the public has been able to encounter what those closest to Robert have known all along.... Robert is more than a doll.

Myrtle Reuter
1722A Von Phister
Key West, Fla 33040

Dear Ms. Reuter:

On behalf of the Key West Art and Historical Society, I
would like to thank you for your generous donation of the
Robert doll belonging to Gene Otto. It is a unique artifact
that will greatly enhance our historical collections.

Enclosed please find your copy of the donation contract.

Again, thank you for thinking of us when making this
donation.

Linda L Spangrud

Linda L Spangrud
Curator

Dear Robert...

I would like to share my story with all the Robert fans. This is my second trip to Key West. My husband and I got married on Smathers Beach last year and returned this year for our one-year wedding anniversary.

I saw Robert last year on the ghost tour and "tested" the picture story about Robert first. I did not ask. Lost all my pics, including our wedding pics the very next morning.

On this trip I brought Robert peppermint candy. My husband and I were the only two in the room with Robert. I showed him the candy and placed it on the wall behind him. The lights in Robert's room all went out for a few seconds – enough time for me and my husband to look at each other in amazement and look back at Robert. My reaction was a teary happiness to know that we were being thanked and shown such a strong reaction to our presence from Robert.

Thank you my friend. We are looking forward to our next visit.

xoxo

Above: Robert takes his first road trip to attend a paranormal conference.

Left: A line of filament was added by museum staff to keep Robert in his chair.

Below: A film crew experiences camera problems while filming a documentary. Camera mishaps are one of many problems blamed on Robert.

INSIDE
ROBERT THE DOLL

PHOTO: ROB O'NEAL

So what makes Robert tick? The answer is anyone's guess, but after eighteen years of investigation I've come to believe that three theories are the most plausible. We know that Emeline and William Abbott were Otto family servants, and we know that Emeline's child was born and died between 1900 and 1910. The first theory says that the doll known as Robert contains the spirit of the child born to Emeline Abbott. The spirit may have entered the doll on its own accord because of similarities between the doll and the human form. There is also the possibility that the child's spirit was contained in the doll with a Voodoo spell performed by its grieving parents.

The second theory is that Robert and Eugene Otto are one and the same. Did Gene project so much energy on the doll as a child that it took on a life of its own? If the stories about the doll are true, it would make sense for Eugene's spirit to join his lifelong companion and reside in the museum with the galleries he helped create. Perhaps his greatest creation of all was the legend of Robert the Doll.

A third possibility is that the doll is nothing more than the cumulative consequences of overactive imaginations. "Uncanny" is a Freudian theory of an instance where something is simultaneously familiar and alien, and therefore seems strange. The individual who has an uncanny experience may find himself being both drawn to and repulsed by an object.

No matter which theory is true, there is no denying the impact of Robert the Doll. This doll, an object usually considered inanimate, influences the thoughts and actions of hundreds of people on a daily basis. He is treated by most as more of a person than a doll, and a veil of fascination and mystery surrounds him.

These are the elements that make a good horror movie, but Robert is a far cry from the creatures you see on the big screen.

As Key West resident Heather Clement said after Robert wreaked havoc on her life:

"Chucky isn't real.

Jason isn't real.

Freddy isn't real.

Robert the Doll... is real."

A NOTE OF CAUTION

It is my hope that you will consider the wilder aspects of Robert the Doll with a healthy dose of skepticism. You certainly should not blindly believe in the abilities of a doll to move on his own and cast curses!

I was skeptical the first time I met Robert, but he wasted no time making me a believer. After years of interaction with Robert, I had reached a certain comfort level, and I thought I was safe. Nothing could have been farther from the truth.

In the process of completing this book, I lost four hard drives. The Apple techs were able to recover everything except the book manuscript each time. Backups of the manuscript also disappeared.

Multiple mediums advised me to purchase a fireproof safe for my valuables while working on this project. I've been told Robert will give me cancer if he doesn't approve. Over the years I have been yanked from my bed, suspended in mid-air and gone through different aspects of possession. I can't say that Robert is responsible, but each incident happened while I was working on the book. If the version you are reading feels rushed at points, it is due to the fact that strange things are happening once again as the writing of this book nears completion.

There is a thin line between possessions and possession. I urge you not to cross that line.

THANKS - CREDITS - SOURCES

THIS BOOK WOULD NOT EXIST AS IT DOES WITHOUT THE MIAMI HERALD, SUN SENTINEL, SOLARES HILL, ISLAND LIFE, KEY WEST CITIZEN, PITTSBURG PRESS, A GHOSTHUNTER'S GUIDE BY ARTHUR MYERS, THE DAILY REPUBLICAN, KEY WESTER MAGAZINE, NEWSPAPER ARCHIVE.COM, ANCESTRY.COM, MONROE COUNTY LIBRARY ARCHIVES, STATE OF FLORIDA ARCHIVES, OTTO FAMILY ARCHIVES, KEY WEST ART & HISTORICAL SOCIETY ARCHIVES, MONROE COUNTY PUBLIC RECORDS, COMMONWEALTH OF MASSACHUSETTES ARCHIVES, KEY WEST CEMETERY ARCHIVES, LIBRARY OF CONGRESS, DIVISION OF COPYRIGHTS, KEY WEST DIRECTORY, THE KEY WEST DRUGGIST, U.S. CENSUS RECORDS, STEIFF ARCHIVES, INTERVIEWS WITH REBEKAH KAUFFMAN @MYSTEIFFLIFE, WILLIAM GEISER, JOE PAIS, SHARON WELLS, TOM HAMBRIGHT, THE ARTIST HOUSE OWNERS & STAFF (1996-PRESENT), PAMELA SEIBER, BETH ROONEY, ANTHONY PICONE, FREDDIE GUIEB, MARIA SHAW LAWSON, DARRYL MEYER, GOODY ESTEVEZ, LAURA FOX, RACHEL CURRAN, DOROTHY DRENNEN, STACEY ROSSEAU, TED MESSIMER, DANIELLE HOLLIDAY, CARLA CABANAS, MIKE MONGO, CLAUDIA PENNINGTON, DENNIS, LINDA AND AGGIE @ THE ARTIST HOUSE, CHRISTOPHER SHULTZ, MICHAEL MARRERO, DINK BRUCE, TOD SLOAN, GREGG MCGRADY, CLINTON CURRY, DEBORAH BELFORD, CINDY PLUME, JAMIE ROUSH, STACEY MITCHELL, HEATHER CLEMENT, GARIN WOLF LARRY STANFORD, THERIAULT'S AUCTION HOUSE, MARKY PIERSON, CORI CONVERTITO, MICHAEL GIEDA, THE KEARNY FAMILY, NICK DOLL & ROB O'NEAL.

MULTIPLE HARD DRIVES AND 4 VERSIONS OF THIS BOOK WERE LOST, AND WITH EACH, NOTES ON SOURCES, CREDITS AND THANKS. IF YOUR NAME OR SOURCE IS NOT LISTED OR PROPERLY CREDITED, ROBERT DID IT. PLEASE CONTACT US SO FUTURE EDITIONS CAN BE CORRECTED. DAVID @PHANTOMPRESS.COM

ABOUT THE AUTHOR

PHOTO: NICK DOLL

David L. Sloan launched his paranormal career in in 1996, founding one of North America's first ghost tours in Key West, Florida. He has South Florida's largest collection of haunted objects, authored a dozen books, studied Santeria and Voodoo, and has dealt first-hand with dark entities and spirit possession.

Sloan was instrumental in Robert the Doll's move from museum storage to permanent display and remains the authority on the haunted history of Key West and The Florida Keys. He is frequently featured on national television and is a regular on several paranormal radio programs.

David lives in Key West and operates Sloan's Ghost Hunt: www.keywestghosthunt.com. Message Sloan directly: david@phantompress.com.

Woman blames fight on Robert the Doll

CITIZEN STAFF

KEY WEST — When all else fails, blame Robert the Doll.

A bickering couple from New York state drew police attention Sunday night after a day of drinking and a tour of East Martello Tower, where Robert the Doll resides.

The girlfriend, 37, of Rochester, N.Y., was jailed on a misdemeanor count of battery.

Robert, a doll cursed with the "black magic of Voodoo," according to www.robertthedoll.org, allegedly haunts the Martello dressed in a crisp white sailor outfit and clutching his Leo Lion stuffed animal.

"Strange things would happen when Robert was around," the site says, urging folks to "Blame it on Robert!" when bizarre incidents crop up. The duo apparently took it to heart.

The boyfriend, 49, of Stafford, N.Y., reportedly called police about 9:30 p.m. saying his girlfriend of five years had punched him in the face. Prior to that, he had tried to evict her from their South Roosevelt Boulevard hotel room, printing out a return plane ticket for her in the lobby.

Police photographed the man's face, noting his upper lip was cut and swollen. The couple parted ways after the girlfriend told officers there was "a tussle," where "hands were thrown." Reports said their speech was slurred.

Afterward, she allegedly texted the boyfriend: "I'm sorry for your lip. I didn't know my capability... All I have to say is, 'Robert did it!'"

She was booked into county jail.

Information in the Crime Report is obtained from reports provided by area law enforcement agencies. If you have information that could help solve a crime in the Keys, call Crime Stoppers, (800) 346-TIPS.

WRITE TO ROBERT

SEND FAN LETTERS, GIFTS, NOTES OF APOLOGY,
AND REQUESTS FOR FORGIVENESS TO:

ROBERT THE DOLL
FORT EAST MARTELLO MUSEUM
3501 SOUTH ROOSEVELT BLVD.
KEY WEST, FL 33040

ORDER ROBERT MERCHANDISE
WWW.ROBERTTHEDOLL.ORG

ORDER AUTOGRAPHED AND PERSONALIZED BOOKS
WWW.ROBERTDIDIT.COM

ALSO AVAILABLE FROM DAVID L. SLOAN

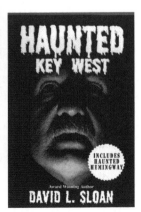

A MESSAGE FROM THE PRESIDENT

THE WHITE HOUSE

WASHINGTON

October 11, 2005

Mr. Robert Otto
Number 43
59151 Overseas Highway
Marathon, Florida 33050

Dear Mr. Otto:

Happy 101st birthday! Laura and I send our best wishes on this joyous occasion.

Your generation has taught Americans the timeless lessons of courage, endurance, and love. By sharing your wisdom and experiences, you continue to serve as a role model for future generations. We hope you enjoy this special day.

May God bless you, and may God continue to bless America.

Sincerely,

George W. Bush